Red
Sea

Protectorate

Aden

Arabian Sea

D1539929

India

Cameroons

Aden

Vietnam

a

Somalia

Thailand

Uganda

Ethiopia

Kenya

N. Borneo

desia

Tanganyika

Malaya

Sarawak

and

Nyasaland

S. Rhodesia

Solomon Is.

Swaziland

Fiji

Solomon Is.

ral Sea

Pacific Ocean

Fiji

New Hebrides

A World
Elsewhere
V.S.O.

By the same author

NEW NIGERIANS

BAGHDAD AND BEYOND

A SEASON IN SARAWAK

HC
60
.D49
1965

A WORLD ELSEWHERE

VOLUNTARY SERVICE OVERSEAS

by Mora Dickson

WITH ILLUSTRATIONS
BY THE AUTHOR

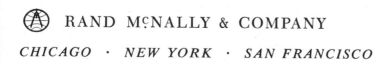

RAND McNALLY & COMPANY

CHICAGO · NEW YORK · SAN FRANCISCO

remembering
MARJORIE McCAW

and in gratitude to
JUNE WALKER

whose devotion and skill
helped to launch this
endeavour

© Mora Dickson 1964

Library of Congress Catalog Card Number: 65-11817

Rand McNally & Company edition, published in the United States and possessions in 1965

Library
State College
Indiana, Penna.

361 D561

c. 1

Contents

Glossary

Attap	Roofing made from palm leaves
Bush	Uncultivated country (Africa) Wild place
Bwana	Master (East and Central Africa)
Bamboli	Local drink (British Guiana)
Boma	District Office (East and Central Africa)
Biltong	Dried meat (Southern Africa)
Compound	Garden or yard
Coolie	Labourer
Corial	Canoe (British Guiana)
Chop	Food (West Africa)
Dhoti	Cloth worn by men (India)
Farrang	Foreigner (Thailand)
Ghee	Cooking oil
Gemsbok	A kind of deer (Bechuanaland)
High Life	West African dance
Ibo	Principal tribe of Eastern Nigeria
Kampong	Village (Malay)
Kgotla	Tribal meeting (Bechuanaland)
Kabaya	Girl's jacket (Malay)
Kumara	Sweet potato (Solomons)
Klong	Canal (Thailand)

GLOSSARY

Kraal	Village (Southern Africa)
Latex	Raw rubber (Far East)
Malawi	Political party (Nyasaland)
	African name for Nyasaland
Masromani	Celebration before communal work (British Guiana)
Pakama	Cloth worn in Thailand
Piai man	Witch-doctor (British Guiana)
Pikipiki	Motor-bicycle (East and Central Africa)
Pana	Sweet potato (Solomons)
Padi	Rice (Far East)
Rondeval	Round house (Southern Africa)
Stelling	Wharf (British Guiana)
Sarong	Cloth worn by men and women (Far East)
Tapai	Local wine (North Borneo)
Ulu	The headwaters of a river (Sarawak)
Vela	Spirit (Solomon Islands)
Wadi	Dry river bed
Yam	Root vegetable (Africa)
Yoruba	Principal tribe in Western Nigeria
Zariba	Thorn branch hedge (Somalia)

PLOUGHING RICE FIELDS

En route to the Solomon Islands

Introduction

PETER

THIS book is about the young volunteer as my husband and I knew him in the early days of Voluntary Service Overseas. It covers a period of roughly two and a half years, from August 1959 to the middle of 1962. I have not included material from the first year's volunteers of 1958–9 because that has, largely, already appeared in print.

No attempt has been made to write a sociological work. I have chosen to present the material as a symposium of the experience of many volunteers, out of which emerges a picture of what it was like to be a volunteer in the years when V.S.O. was still a revolutionary idea. I have used only Christian names and, in one or two cases not identified, pseudonyms; and I have not attempted to pinpoint background or schooling. Though these may have affected superficially how the job was tackled the experience was essentially that of an adolescent 'finding' himself through being accepted by the adult world as a man, and required to do a man's work; and as such the experience was common to all.

A small, but increasing, number of the volunteers were girls. I have indicated in the text where this is so, but for convenience in general I have spoken of the individual volunteer as 'he'.

The important factor to remember when reading this book is that the average age of the volunteers was eighteen–nineteen. A very few, notably the apprentices, could be twenty-one or twenty-two; one or two exceptions were just under eighteen: but it was as

9

'teenagers', that much-maligned age group, that these young people went overseas.

This is not my book but the volunteers', without whom Voluntary Service Overseas would have been impossible. With their permission I have used their letters to us to recreate their experience, and I have not attempted to expand the picture outside the range of this material.

MURAT RESETTLEMENT SCHEME NORTH BORNEO

Voluntary
Service
Overseas

JOHN

In September 1958 ten young men left Britain for Sarawak, three flew to Nigeria and two set off for Ghana. All were eighteen years old and had just finished their schooling, but found themselves, due to pressure on higher educational establishments, with twelve months to spare before they could go on to the next stage of their training. They were the spearhead of the scheme which was Voluntary Service Overseas.

At that time the idea that volunteers of this age should spend a year working in countries where help was desperately needed was revolutionary, and my husband, whose concept it was, had spent the two preceding years trying to persuade those in positions of influence and authority, both in Britain and overseas, even to consider the possibility. It was hard work. At every point apparently excellent reasons were advanced as to why it was impossible to send a youngster to work in the under-developed world. There were weeks, even months, when only our own convictions, based on personal experience in Africa and Asia, kept us going.

The difficulties were threefold: to open up genuine opportunities where young volunteers would be acceptable; to find sufficient

11

financial backing to launch such a scheme; and to gain the kind of support in Britain without which it seemed that it would be impossible to send out youngsters from this country to work in territories which had been, or still were, associated with it. Of the three this latter was, probably, the most difficult. The finding of the volunteers themselves was not a problem.

However, months of patient work, and eventually the help and interest of a few people who had become caught up in the idea, made it possible to choose fifteen young men to go out in the autumn of 1958. They came, equally, from grammar and public schools, and they went, in this first instance, to men working in schools and development schemes overseas who were personally known to my husband and myself.

Their travel was financed from Britain, either directly through the gifts of Trusts and Foundations, or indirectly through the generosity of shipping companies who granted free passages. Their living expenses were a charge on the agency or government to which they were accredited overseas, and a small amount of pocket-money, about £1 a week, was also paid them by their employers. The volunteers themselves gave their services free and they provided their own clothing. They all went for a period of twelve months.

Once within a country it quickly became obvious that they could, in fact, give valuable help, and that they could, and did, behave in a sensible and responsible manner. None of the fears which had been expressed to us beforehand proved to have any foundation. The next year the requests jumped to sixty, and a great many more countries, other than the original three, had become involved. For the next three years the graph climbed steadily, and by 1961, inspired by the success of these first volunteers, many other countries, notably America, had begun to think in terms of the volunteer overseas. V.S.O. had also widened its field to take in the young apprentice and the police cadet, and since the second year had accepted an increasing number of girls.

NIGERIAN WOMAN

12

In one way, however, V.S.O. remained unique. The age of its volunteers was a feature about which we felt strongly, but it was one that no other endeavour of this kind had the courage to copy. There were good reasons for choosing this particular age and we had not done so lightly or without serious discussion.

In a period in which the whole status of countries was changing with great rapidity, and when a whole paternalistic pattern was dissolving, it was important that any fresh wave of overseas workers going out from Britain should have, and should demonstrably be seen to have, a new conception of racial partnership. And because there happened also to be a world-wide awakening among the young which, to some extent, divorced them from their own adult compatriots, it seemed that the young could speak to the young across barriers of nationality or colour in a way which it had increasingly become more difficult for any other age group to do. There was a language of youth which it might well be possible to use for freer communication of ideas and understanding, but the years in which this language was really a living one were quite few and our experience was that even in the early twenties it began to be bedevilled by inhibition and misconstruction.

At this age, eighteen–nineteen, it was a genuine fact that the volunteer was gaining as much from the country he served as he was giving. He was being offered an experience in the difficulties of community and nation building which was invaluable to him and which he could, probably, never get in his own affluent society. He appreciated this and was willing to be the recipient of this gift. Psychologically this was of very great importance both to his own attitude and the attitude of the country which accepted him. There was no condescension on either side; both gave and both received.

This was the moment, probably the first adult job in surroundings which accepted him completely on his own merits, when there was a freshness and warmth about the young volunteer which not only opened doors to him – it opened hearts also. He was prepared to be taught as well as to teach, to gain friends as well as to give friendship and this was an attitude which the overseas world had not often seen in Britons.

His qualifications might still be humble ones, but his youth gave an alert and incisive edge to his mind and body which made him quick to absorb new situations and skilful in adapting his abilities to meet them. He was prepared for discipline, in a way which did

13

not come easily to the older volunteer, while at the same time being responsive to any need for initiative. And he came without encumbrances, no family to worry over, unburdened by financial commitments, ready to go anywhere and to turn his hand to anything, valuable qualities in countries where life was fluid and often uncertain.

One other asset belonged essentially to the young volunteer. Between two sure commitments—his school and university or college, his school and a job, on release from his firm—he was in a situation that freed him from anxieties about the future to give his whole heart and mind to the job in hand. Not for him the anxious weeks towards the middle of his service when he began to wonder if, back at home, contemporaries were cutting him out of his chosen career; not for him the difficulties of decision about what the next step should be, this was already decided before he left, and, although this decision might later be changed in the light of his experience, there was no need for him, while still on the job, to be casting about for comforting advice as to his own future.

This then was the background to the correspondence of some three hundred and fifty volunteers out of which this book has been created.

The Letters

COLIN

WHEN Voluntary Service Overseas originally came into being, and the first volunteers had been despatched overseas, it became apparent that there was a need for continuing communication. We wanted very much to know what would happen to them; the real job began with the goodbyes at London Airport or some railway terminus, for us as well as for them. This was the moment on which all depended. Now we would discover whether the theories which we had propounded, the ideas which we had discussed and dreamed about, were valid. We had entrusted these ideas to the young men who had gone out, for them to use as they felt fit, for them to adapt to their own personalities and situations, and we were intensely curious and deeply interested to know whether we had equipped them well.

On this knowledge, too, depended all future developments. We saw the departure of the very first volunteers not as a climax but as the first step in something that might grow to proportions which we could not at that moment visualise. It was upon these individuals

15

that this growth depended—and we recognised this; it was fundamental in our briefing of them that they, too, came to this realisation.
So the scheme, in reality, depended entirely on its volunteers, and
they knew themselves to be as much concerned in its discovery, its
growth and its foundation-building as we were ourselves. For this
reason also communication was essential to them. It was important
not only that they should do a job, but that they should be able to
assess it, to philosophise about it with ourselves, and through us
with each other. They went out to work separately, but their strength
would lie in their knowledge that they were not, in fact, separated;
each was a vital, independent, responsible unit, whose knowledge
contributed to the whole, whose views were heard and respected,
whose value to the whole was unquestioned.

They were all young. Although they were more than capable of
doing a man-size job—and the whole concept of V.S.O. rested on
the conviction that they were the responsible people which they
later showed themselves to be—there was, nevertheless, no con-
tradiction in recognising that they were also very young. They stood
at a threshold, and the life that they were going out to meet would be
very strange to them. They had never before cut so completely the
bonds which joined them to home, school, factory, friends: the safe,
same, steady way of life that they had always known. They would
discover, many of them, how young they really were, and they
would need support and signposts to help them when they made this
discovery. Of course they would have all this from their parents and
their friends; many would find that more people really cared for them
than they had realised in the casual contacts of every day. But there
was a special relationship that could be filled only by someone who
knew a little of what it was that they were going out to find, who was
removed from a close family connection, and in whom they had
confidence. In the beginning it was only ourselves who fulfilled
these qualifications and who had the time to devote to this.

Much of what we felt is implicit in this word confidence. To
each one of the volunteers this was an outstanding experience, and
they took very seriously their first fully adult job. They could write
of it to their families—indeed they did so—but all the family's love
and interest could not prevent inhibitions, sometimes a feeling of not
being taken quite seriously, maybe a notion that 'they wouldn't
understand', which might make it impossible to write home at some
moment of crisis when help was particularly needed. The family,

proud and impressed, did its best to communicate interest and assistance, but if they had never been out of Europe it became, of necessity, very difficult to convey to them the real atmosphere, or the real problems, facing their son. In these circumstances it was of vital importance that each volunteer should be able to write to us, in a personal and ordinary way—in other words divorced from the atmosphere that might smack of reporting to an office—and that they should feel confident not only of our understanding, because we had ourselves done this kind of work in many countries, but of getting in reply a personal and individual letter. This was a channel of communication which was kept always open; through which, at any time and on any problem each volunteer could feel that he had direct access to what help and advice we could give, and a real stake in shaping the future of the scheme.

The problems differed from boy to boy, from country to country, from job to job. It was not that, however, which made us feel that some kind of circular letter would be a mistake. I can perhaps best describe what we felt by saying that the strength of the scheme, as we conceived it, lay in individual importance within a unified whole. The volunteers were vital, but it was not as cogs that they were vital; it was as people, all different. We never tried to enforce a pattern on them, what we attempted to do was to give them certain basic fundamentals of integrity, truth, faith and confidence, humility and humour, and a variety of tools from which they could choose those which best suited their own talents and the situation which they found; and to send them out with the knowledge that they had our complete confidence in their ability to deal with the work for which they had been chosen, and with the difficulties, not according to some formula which we laid down but by the light of the basic truths and their own judgement, kindliness and common sense. When they wrote for help they received back, as far as possible, some practical suggestions, the knowledge that they were not unique in their trouble, but, above all, our complete confidence in their own ability to come through the crisis, to face it—perhaps to resolve it, but not necessarily. As I understood it this was the help they needed. Each and every one was, in himself or herself, capable of meeting the situations they did meet, each one had immense powers within himself to draw on; where they faltered sometimes was in lacking the confidence to do so, or in fearing that they would not be considered adequate. The knowledge that we trusted them, that we

17

recognised their individual limitations but had no doubt at all that these were wider than they themselves suspected, was very often all that was needed to set them on the way to a local solution.

CHINESE WOMAN WORKER

MICHAEL

Briefing

OVER the period of time represented by the first three years of V.S.O., autumn 1958 to summer 1961, certain factors became clear about the training of volunteers. Because the work was rapidly expanding with, as yet, inadequate funds, it was constantly overtaking its hard-pressed staff. This was not a bad thing, serving to keep the scheme from hardening into a cut-and-dried mould and permeating us at the centre of things with a spirit of pioneering and improvisation similiar to that which activated the volunteers in the field — a fact which brought ourselves and the volunteers closer together than we might otherwise have been — but it did have the disadvantage that there was little time left to experiment with training courses.

A more important factor, however, was inherent in the situation of the volunteers. The majority were school-leavers, who, until a very short while before they were due to leave, were fully occupied at school, sometimes with important exams. Their time, too, was therefore limited. Similarly firms, releasing apprentices for the comparatively long period of a year overseas, were not particularly anxious, at this experimental stage, to add to it a further period of training.

These considerations made us look in other directions for ways of preparing the young volunteer for his service overseas, and it seemed that one way to do this was to throw the onus of training back on the volunteer; to demand self-training which gave, as a valuable by-product to the actual skills acquired, an initial exercise in initiative, tact, perseverance and dealing with adults in authority. Many a volunteer destined for Borneo or Bechuanaland made his first faltering steps in self-discipline and responsibility contacting those who could help him to prepare himself in Birmingham or Beaconsfield.

What had started as an emergency measure contained, we felt, much that was valuable. The boy who was lost in his home town of Nuneaton was not going to be of much assistance in the strange one of Nairobi. And so, out of experience, these briefing notes were compiled by my husband, and in 1961 each volunteer received a copy of them as soon as he was finally selected. They contained everything that had, in essence, been said to the earlier volunteers and so they are relevant to all the letters during this period.

Many of the practical and physical instructions contained in the notes are not of importance here, but certain sections are valuable, giving, as they do, a clear idea of the concepts that the volunteer took with him of his own position and function in relation to those who were sending him and the government, mission or agency which he would serve overseas. Some of the emphases in the volunteer's own letters can be better understood if they are related back to his 'briefing notes' which represented the thinking of those who sent him combined with and based on the experience of the first to go abroad.

Guidance and Instruction for those selected as Volunteers

Please read these notes very carefully. Your year under Voluntary Service Overseas is likely to be the most important thing you have yet undertaken in your life. The more care and thought you can give to your preparation, the better. These notes are the product of the experience of volunteers in some thirty different countries; on that account, one must, to some extent, generalise. What may be important in the Falkland Islands may not be applicable in Fiji.

20

Appearance: Your appearance is very important indeed; do not assume because the country to which you are going is sometimes referred to as 'under-developed' that this relieves you of the responsibility for looking neat and tidy. It is essential that you should remain clean-shaven; any incipient beard will mark you as being peculiar or even weird; better, not only for hygiene, cleanliness and appearance, a 'crew-cut' rather than long hair—no matter how difficult it might be to find a proper barber. The younger generation in the West Indies, in Africa, and most especially in Asia, are definitely fastidious about their appearance and the cleanliness of their clothes. School pupils, even in the most remote parts of the South East Asian territories, manage to appear daily in most excellently washed clothes. It must regretfully be stated that some of our volunteers have too often made an impression on the local people of being slovenly to the point of dirtiness.

Hospitality: Almost certainly at the beginning of your stay you will be a guest in someone's house. In some cases this may be continued or be repeated on many occasions; do please show appreciation of the fact that you are a guest involving your host and staff in additional trouble, this is tremendously important. Years at a boarding school or camping holidays or visits to relatives may not have made you aware of the trouble that a guest can cause in a stranger's house. None of these people who accommodate you has been forced to do so. Do try to make it a pleasure for them—even if their bathroom is so very different from the one you have at home and the food ditto. A letter of thanks to your hosts will sweeten life generally.

It is probable that you may find yourself established in your own household with responsibility for ordering food, having your food prepared, etc. It is possible that you may never have been responsible for running a household of your own at all! Well, do your best; local residents will probably give you advice if you request it. Books have been written on this subject and we will not try to summarise any advice here but, remember, it is not too late even now to go into training at home during the few weeks that are left to you—under the guidance and instruction of your mother!

The fact that you have been living for many years surrounded by a well-kept household and a well-kept kitchen is no guarantee that when suddenly confronted with the responsibility for running these things on your own you will really know what to do. By the way, can you wash and iron your own clothes? Perhaps you may not have to — perhaps, again, you will have to. This could be as important as 'Advanced' levels!

.   .   .   .   .

Textbooks: Many volunteers will be going to teach in schools. If you are in this category do not be in a hurry to get rid of your own school textbooks before leaving. A textbook (or even your own lecture notes) with which you have grown very familiar can be of great help to you in preparing lessons and giving out exercises, even if it does not happen to be the textbook used in the particular school to which you are attached; in which case you may gain added prestige for the apparent ease with which you appear in the class-room with well-formulated questions and exercises!

First-aid: You were warned about this in the brochure about Voluntary Service Overseas. Are you proficient now? If not, you have a few weeks to get proficient in it. We are not thinking so much about your own safety of life or limb as your capacity to teach first-aid to others, in a sensible and stimulating way. You are strongly advised to take out a small handbook, preferably well illustrated, to help you to give instructions.

Swimming: We are assuming, as a matter of course, that not only can you swim adequately but that you have taken the trouble to learn something about life-saving (again other people's lives, not yours). If your place of work is on a river or the sea, the probability is that the local youth already swim like fishes, but life-saving is a Western concept and a Western technique; see to it that it is one more skill which you can communicate to others.

Boxing: You do not care especially about boxing? But you are about to become an educationist, at least for a year, and this means your having to get young people to do things which they may not particularly want to undertake; indeed, this might be regarded as the very heart of education. Schooling yourself to do something that you may not take to naturally can be as good a preparation as any for learning to teach others. West Africa is the cradle of British

Empire featherweight champions. You are not being asked to offer yourself as a victim or sacrifice for other people's fists; you are being asked to help a group of schoolboys or young club members to take up something of this kind, perhaps more friendly and sportingly than might otherwise have been the case.

Football: If you come from a rugger-playing background, swallow your pride and join in soccer with the local boys. If you come from a soccer-playing background, then you should be prepared even to harden your soles and play as the local boys do!

Music: However amateurish you may be, do try to take some instrument to play; obviously, a grand piano or a double-bass will absorb your 44-lb air allowance, but a recorder (not the tape-recorder kind) or even a mouth-organ (and, not least, comb-and-paper) may contribute mutually to happiness in your project. Forget our national characteristic of shyness regarding singing. In the West Indies and in most parts of Africa it is music which really unlocks people. If you can get your group to sing on their way to work, sing even during their work and sing on their return from work, you will be amazed at what can be achieved. Take some songbooks with you; they need not be of the too serious 'Olde English' folk-tune kind; even the songs from 'My Fair Lady' can be a hit in many parts of the world. The writer of these notes remembers hearing 'Que Sera, Sera' sung by the local boys as they cut grass in a jungle clearing on the Sarawak-Indonesian frontier.

Prayers: Obviously, much might be written on the question of religion and your responsibility during your service overseas. We will content ourselves here by saying that you are very likely to find yourself expected to take prayers; do not be dismayed; you will find that you will be able to rise to the occasion; but you might be glad if you had taken the trouble to take out with you a small prayerbook in straightforward English.

Hobbies: You may think this a rather juvenile word ... do not despise it. If you have yourself a keen interest or pursuit, take the wherewithal to enjoy it (e.g. a telescope if you are interested in the stars) because there will certainly be 'grey' days, if not 'black' days, and you will want to seek the consolation of your hobby, and you should try to share this with the local youth. If you are anything of a conjuror, then take your equipment and be prepared to do your stuff. If you are not, you might, nevertheless, try to get a little book on match tricks, for example, from which endless amusement can be derived.

Sports and Games: Get some little book or books on games, other than those in which you may be experienced. You might find yourself in some spot where there is not room for a proper game of football or conditions are so primitive that there is not even a football itself. There are many first-class games that can, nevertheless, be played in these circumstances. Or you may find yourself in parts of South East Asia where the local people play basketball with something approaching brilliance. Do not be standoffish—join in with them and ask them to teach you. The Boy Scouts' Association sell excellent books on what are called 'wide games', which are outdoor games. There may not be the long winter evenings (unless you are going to Labrador or the Falklands) but in the Tropics darkness will fall at round about the same time every evening. If it is a school at which you are working, the children may have evening studies to do; they and you may have to contend with rather inadequate lighting. You may, perhaps, think that they are excessively preoccupied with examinable subjects to the exclusion of other more normal and leisurely pursuits; anyway, try and encourage indoor games. There are two or three lightweight books which will give you many ideas for games for brawny boys, games for brainy boys, games for large groups, games for small groups, etc. etc.; properly and imaginatively presented, such games can have a real educational value.

Book-keeping: Can you keep simple accounts? You might find yourself landed with the accounts for the whole school or for a small club; to be able to show how to keep reasonable accounts may be of considerable importance to the small community to which you are attached. Do not go to a Chartered Accountant or he will be professionally offended at the notion of your trying to learn the fundamentals of his craft in two easy lessons. Go around to a local builder or shopkeeper who has perforce to keep accounts—or the school bursar might help.

Youth organisations: If you are a Queen's Scout or something of that kind, of course, you will be taking your uniform and other equipment. You may find it quite difficult to adapt Scouting so

Library
State College
Indiana, Penna.

361 D561
c. 1

that it really fulfils local needs but, of course, you will do your best.
If you were once, in your dim and distant youth, a Scout but have
long since ceased to be active, then reflect seriously about the immense value which you can be in helping Scouting overseas. There
is no room whatever for scepticism or sophistication in the attitude
of a V.S.O. volunteer. However, you may find that a Youth Club,
possibly a mixed Youth Club, may be more of what is needed in the
particular circumstances. Do you know anything about how to start
this? Or, perhaps more imaginatively, how to revive one or to keep
it going when interest appears to flag? You have only a few weeks
in which to learn!

Building: Can you lay a foundation, or use a plumb-line or even
a compass or a spirit level, or mix cement or lay bricks? If you have
any talent whatever in this direction, polish it up. Even if you
find yourself working in a European community, you might be able
to get some of the local boys to do a spot of building or rebuilding
in a slum area. If you have any carpentry talents and any manual
skills in that direction, be prepared to use them. Volunteers from
industry should take with them both any technical manuals and such
tools as they might need.

P.T. or Gymnastics: The hard-pressed headmaster of any school
overseas is likely to be more than willing to hand over the schedule
for physical education to a bright new willing arrival from Britain.
Can you make P.T. go with a 'Zip' and retrieve it from the frightful
limbo of 'bird-flapping' exercises in which it languishes in all too
many schools overseas? Can you do gymnastic 'tumbling' or agility
work or pyramids? Can you devise assault courses (civilian)? Can
you put on some kind of demonstration or display? Some of our
volunteers have made a tremendous success of this. Can you?
Consult your P.E. instructor, or seek advice from the Y.M.C.A.

Dancing: Though you
may be surprised at the
degree of enthusiasm
shown even in the most
improbable and remote
places for English ball-
room dancing in which
there is no reason why
you should not take part,

PUBLIC WORKS DEPARTMENT, NORTH BORNEO

remember that V.S. stands for Voluntary Service—not Victor Sylvester. Square dancing, Scottish country dancing and the like can go down very well indeed—and we would advocate these in preference. Anyway, take booklets that can help you.

Play-acting: Whilst some senior secondary schools in more advanced territories may put on Shakespeare, you may find that play-acting has to be reconceived afresh. It may not be so much a case of formally rehearsing printed parts of a play by Galsworthy or W.W. Jacobs but of introducing a note of mimicry and drama even into formal lessons. You saw somebody doing something reprehensible in the dormitory or the public highway yesterday: you do not deliver a lecture on the subject but you somehow dramatise the incident so as to bring it home. Most peoples in these more distant parts of the world have an inherent capacity for improvisation, amounting almost to genius.

Teaching: If in the fortnight or so that is left to you, you can persuade a skilled and/or sympathetic master at school to take you into his confidence and show you some of the 'tricks of his trade' (e.g. blackboard techniques), how to ask questions, etc. etc., you will not regret it. The Ministry of Education has just extended the period of teacher training from two to three years; you cannot condense this into two weeks, but it is just possible that a little learning may not be so dangerous as some suppose. You may even find yourself teaching English in a French-speaking territory.

Girl volunteers may find themselves teaching sewing and simple embroidery, and it would be an asset to be able to make your own paper patterns for dressmaking. If you are good at these skills take fresh stock of your knowledge and make notes or collect samples to carry with you. If you are not very skilled, try to learn the basics of mending and sewing before you go.

Work with Women: If you are likely to be dealing with women's groups it would be worth your while to find out how groups in this country are run. Have a talk with someone connected with the Women's Institutes, the Y.W.C.A., the Townswomen's Guild or other organisation and get some idea of their constitution, finance, programme, etc. The situation overseas will be totally different, but, at least you will have some idea of the way groups function from which to begin to adapt your suggestions.

The position of women in the countries to which you will go differs very much from the situation in your own daily life at home. There may be many things which you would do without thinking which might be abhorrent to them. For instance, in some places parents would not dream of letting their daughters join a mixed youth club. Try to gain some real insight into the social traditions and background of the girls with whom you are working and adapt any new ideas you may want to introduce to fit in with them. Your work stands a much greater chance of being a success if it is a development grafted on to a local custom and not a completely strange notion superimposed from outside. It is wiser not to wear shorts, both men and women would consider them shockingly immodest, though they would be too polite to tell you so, and your whole effort to help might well be invalidated by this. Remember that your appearance is important not only to you personally but because it may be from you that people form their opinions of Europeans; so try not to offend their sense of propriety and decency.

Your Home: The people amongst whom you work are likely to be curious about you yourself. If you had had sitting or working beside you in the classroom or workshop over the last term or year a young African, you would have become curious about him: not only the texture of his hair, the colour of the palms of his hands, but the kind of home that he came from, his family, etc. In the same way, there will be an interest in your own background. Satisfy this — and turn it to good educational account. Take with you photographs of your own home and family and parents, including a snap of the dog (for the notion of keeping a pet in the house, eating specially prepared food, may in itself be a matter for wonderment in some overseas countries). Take any literature about your home town (the kind of brochure which you get from the Town Clerk). Take as much material about your school or your firm, a group photograph, the school or house magazine. Even your old school cap could be a useful 'exhibit' around which you could build quite an instructive talk about school discipline, the proper role of a prefect, esprit de corps, etc.

About Britain: When you talk about life in Britain, bear in mind that it is the familiar things (which may nevertheless be slightly different) which interest people — not the exotic or exceptional. The London Underground, the Piccadilly escalator, the Dounray Reactor or the

Jodrell Bank telescope are unlikely to mean anything to people living in the forest or the humbler back streets of some small coastal town in a far-away country. A typical Saturday in your life, however, could well absorb them. The fact that letters come tumbling through a hole in the outer door twice a day will amaze people for whom letters are something that have to be collected from a post office after a long trek. The fact that our houses have an 'upstairs' or a built-in w.c., will surprise some people. After all, the notion of an open fireplace is regarded as distinctly quaint by some Americans, and most countries of Western Europe are accustomed to central heating.

Photos: Take with you a good many picture postcards, preferably in colour, of the kind that tourists buy in Trafalgar Square, showing a London policeman, the Changing of the Guard, the Queen on horseback. These can be judiciously used as presents to be awarded either to those whose friendship you have won or who have helped you in some way, or as a small prize at a Scout camp, a school concert or some other function. Take with you several photographs of yourself (small size or even passport size). At the outset they can be useful in obtaining driving licences or identity cards: at the end of your service you may wish to give them away to your friends, if you have any left! (Interpret this how you will.)

Forging Links: Do your utmost to work up a link with the school or community where you are working and your school at home, or the youth group to which you are attached and some group to which you belong in Britain (and the same could apply to an apprentice school here in this country). You may regard the idea of 'pen pals' as something slightly juvenile: nevertheless, if you can get some of the younger people back in Britain writing out to some of the people with whom you are working, it is likely to be of mutual benefit. But a link can consist of something more than just an exchange of letters. Some schools in Britain have actually helped their volunteer overseas with equipment and books. Nothing but good can come out of this kind of contact.

Stories: Telling stories is still the world's greatest indoor entertainment amongst the many millions who have no idea of radio, TV, bridge or the evening newspaper. There is a Director of Education who, when he goes on official journeys to the remote village communities, tells a story every evening from Herodotus. I have watched the faces of the elders and the children as he says, 'And then on the fifth day the King said "Let the two guards be brought before me who have let the robbers enter my palace. Let their hands be painted with some..."' Stories which have gripped simple rural folk two and a half thousand years ago in Ancient Greece can still grip simple rural folk in other parts of the world today.

School and the Community: If it is a good thing for schools in Britain to take an interest in the community around them, it is no less desirable overseas. Can you get the senior pupils to undertake a social survey (do you know how to undertake one yourself?). There are ways of leading up to this. For example you might express surprise at your inability to find a guide book in a local bookshop (you may have difficulty in finding a local bookshop). This might lead you to suggest that pupils themselves undertake the production of a guide book. This would involve sketches, maps, photographs, descriptions, some local history, etc., leading up the actual reproduction of the guide book in some way or other.

If, as may be likely, you are serving in a multiracial community then you have added opportunities. In North Borneo, for example, you might get the Bajaos to make a study of the Malays, the Malays of the Chinese, and the Chinese of perhaps the most curious element of all—the British! In this way you have not only provided an exercise in ingenuity, local civic sense, etc., but you have conveyed indirectly the idea that each of these races has its own way of life, pride, etc., yet altogether they form one nation. You do not have to be reminded that this is probably one of the most important things in the world today, above all in multiracial countries.

Exploration and Social Service: Adventure is what is unusual. For a boy living in Newcastle it is an adventure to camp out beneath the stars and make his own fire. For a boy whose home has been a village in Nigeria, adventure lies in getting to the township, riding in a lorry, going up in a lift for the first time, even sitting at a typewriter. Having had to gather sticks for a fire during his early youth, this conveys no magic to him at all. It is something he wants to escape from. This is one reason why British youth movements have some difficulty in spreading their message effectively in some countries. But this is not to say that you have to resign yourself to the impossibility of attracting the senior young people to undertake adventurous projects in rural areas or in the slums. To an extent which may seem very strange against a background of contemporary British life, awaking youth to a sense of nationhood and the challenge of building up their own country is not an impossible task. If it can be represented to the local youth that some village will only get a small dam or a new market-place or a clinic if they go and help build it, then a good response is certainly not out of the question.

Some of the local young people may think that climbing mountains is not much 'fun'. Remember that we in Europe held mountains in awe up to about 1790, until the influence of Rousseau and the Romantic Movement. In some instances it may be necessary to contrive a mundane purpose for such an expedition, in the same way that university graduates (and even those a little older) always give to any of their expeditions (which you and I shrewdly assume to be undertaken principally for the fun of the thing) some impressive-looking scientific purpose. The things that come indirectly out of such expeditions or projects may be more important than their ostensible purpose. Town boys get to realise the conditions under which rural people live. Students of one race, by being the recipients of the hospitality of villagers of another race, begin to think of what constitutes a sense of citizenship. Seeing you humping your own pack, and possibly even helping with theirs may even give them an insight into the make-up of white men.

.   .   .   .   .

Remember that you represent, above all, an export of ideas. Other material deficiencies can easily be remedied on the spot, but if you run short of ideas then you are a dead loss. That is why we advocate your taking as many little instructional booklets as possible of the 'Things to Make' and 'How to do it' variety, to help you in whatever you may be trying to teach. Even if you are a bronze medallist or a 'dab' at carpentry, first-aid or P.T., a small illustrated manual can assist you to 'put it over' more effectively.

Languages: In many parts of West Africa English is widely spoken and understood. In the Caribbean, English is the mother tongue. But elsewhere volunteers should make a real effort to learn a lingua-franca, Swahili in East Africa (or Chinyanja in Nyasaland and

Chibemba in Northern Rhodesia) is not difficult; in Malaya, Sarawak and North Borneo, an ability to speak a little Malay—which is simple to learn—will make life so much more worthwhile. Elsewhere, particularly perhaps in India or Arab-speaking countries, the task may be considerably harder. But do make an effort, and if you are going by sea, consult us about a language primer to study during the voyage.

Loyalties: You will have a loyalty towards those amongst whom you work directly: here your age may be an asset, enabling you to win their friendship. But you yourself are quite likely to be in a position of authority meriting respect if not actually exacting discipline. This is never a simple relationship—but it is a situation familiar to a prefect in a good school.

If you are posted in pairs, bear in mind that there will doubtless be occasions when the other volunteer will be sharing one thought at least with you: How on earth did he (or she) come to be selected for V.S.O.? This is a relationship that may be important for your happiness and success: cultivate it.

But you will also owe an allegiance to whoever is in charge of your particular project, whether that person be of British origin or of local nationality. It is, generally, out-of-the-ordinary people who devote themselves to schemes of social service in remote places: furthermore, long years of such work in overseas territories may result in their being out of touch with contemporary youth in this country. It is just conceivable that with their experience they may be more often right than you are. Bear these points in mind, if and when you are inclined to be impatient of what you may regard sometimes as old-fashioned or odd attitudes, and recall Arthur Balfour's words: 'None of us is infallible—not even the youngest of us.' Misunderstanding between young and old is not something peculiar to Lagos or Labrador: it is encountered also in Liverpool and London. These people have asked for your help; you have volunteered; do not let them down.

Some volunteers may find themselves in places where there are a few Europeans: others may be posted to centres where there is quite a large resident white population. Under such circumstances volunteers may feel that they want to identify themselves with the indigenous people, and have as little to do with white social life as possible; or they may find themselves naturally accepting invitations to European houses and parties. To steer a middle course between being thought a crank or a clubman calls for a considerable amount of common sense. But the volunteer in this rather tricky situation does have a tremendous opportunity to act as a catalyst. What kind of a catalyst? Surely it is to 'spark' amongst the local white youth a reciprocal readiness to take part in social service projects alongside the indigenous people. If volunteers succeed in getting some of the young settlers in, say, Rhodesia or Kenya, to join with them in their work in African reserves or clubs, it will not be by adopting any 'holier than thou' attitude or smug condemnation of apartheid, but because they can make their work seem an adventure in service.

.   .   .   .   .

Morale: Volunteers who go to replace others, report at first that they find being constantly compared with their predecessors unnerving. 'I'm tired of hearing how wonderfully John (or Joan) coped with this or that,' they write. This is inevitable. Do not let this get you down: you will presently be making your own impact.

A name that means a lot today in parts of South East Asia and in the United States is that of Dr Dooley, a young American who devoted himself, after Korea, to medical work in Laos and Vietnam. On his last leave the following lines by the poet Robert Frost were constantly in his mind, and they might be in your's too:

> The woods are lovely, dark and deep,
> But I have promises to keep,
> And miles to go before I sleep,
> And miles to go before I sleep,

COUNTRY BOATS, EAST PAKISTAN

CHAPTER I

The Beginning

IAN

OUR first view of a volunteer was usually at a selection board. Both boys and boards came in all shapes and sizes, and each could be nervous of the other. On the whole, however, most volunteers who came before a board, neatly brushed and dressed, answers polished beforehand, were confident and articulate and fairly certain of their own ability to undertake whatever might be required.

Once selected there would be a further interview for briefing. Here, too, the volunteer would arrive jaunty and sure of himself, the more so this time as the decision had been made and he felt secure in his acceptance. Occasionally it was hard to recognise as the same boy the smart, courteous, deferential youth who had been selected and the faintly scruffy, extremely cheerful youngster who now appeared to get his instructions.

This air of relaxed confidence did not last. Sometimes it was shattered almost immediately by the sharp reminder that volunteers were expected to take extensive notes and the sudden discovery that the letting down of his guard had also meant leaving pencil and note-book at home! Suitably sobered, and provided with the necessary material, business then began. As it continued and my husband gradually unfolded not only the actual work involved but also the philosophy behind doing this sort of job at all, the boy in front of him became visibly more aware of his own shortcomings and appre-hensive about his ability to measure up to what was required of him. At the same time the realisation that very high standards were being set tightened his resolve and gave him, perhaps for the first time in the whole procedure, a recognition that the real enterprise which lay before him was far removed from the schoolboy dream of adventure

33

or even the vague desire to help which had originally brought him to volunteer. The reality was both more mundane and more demanding than he had realised; he was no longer the schoolboy, with allowances made for this fact by the adult world, he was a young man aware that he was without the defence or the excuse of special privilege. When, at the end, my husband asked, as he invariably did, 'Well, do you want to withdraw?' the answer always came soberly and with the recognition that it was not a contract to be entered into lightly: 'No, sir.'

Occasionally there was a boy who felt none of this; who contained within himself a self-confidence which hid from him the real extent of the difficulties which he would encounter. We were always nervous when we met one of these, and experience bore out our own feelings that the boy who felt himself equal to any situation was, in fact, rarely so when it came to the test. Over the years we sent out with a great deal more confidence the nervous, white-faced, uncertain volunteer than we did the jaunty, confident, suave one.

When the time came for the final goodbyes, and the last physical tie was cut with home and headquarters, it was often a strangely shrunk, very young figure who peered out sadly through the window of the airport bus, or leant silently out of the railway carriage door, torn between regret at ever having volunteered at all and a conviction that everything must get better from this moment because nothing could surely be much worse.

They travelled in many different ways. In these early years money was not easy to come by, and a rapidly expanding scheme demanded, if it were to go forward at all, that every possible avenue of help be explored. To this end we approached every organisation connected with transport of any kind to countries overseas. They responded magnificently; in all the first years no shipping company that was asked for help in kind ever refused, and the Services too gave their assistance freely.

So it happened that in the months of August and September, which was the despatching season for V.S.O., young men were leaving London for widely varied destinations, travelling by tanker, cargo boat, passenger ship, aeroplane, Royal Navy, Royal Air Force, and many other craft.

Some of these small groups we saw off personally. Sean, Fred, Graham and Ian all left for the Far East, for destinations eventually in Sarawak and North Borneo, by way of Liverpool Street Station,

London. They were to travel on an oil tanker to be boarded at Rotterdam, but somehow at 6 p.m. on a temperate summer evening in a dingy London station all this seemed impossibly exotic.

Fred had only got there at all by the skin of his teeth. Two days before he rang up to say that he just wanted to check that it was all right not to be vaccinated because he had been done as a baby! The resulting panic when he discovered that it was by no means all right had cast Fred, his family and ourselves into a flurry of activity to persuade authorities that a vaccination could be obtained in a fraction of the usual time. On the platform at the station Fred, surrounded by all his family, had not quite recovered from it. Tall and lanky, clutching an assortment of luggage which included a musical instrument, he looked as though he might well have left some more vital preparations undone. The other three eyed each other and us silently. Graham and Ian, who came from the same school, had said their goodbyes earlier, and now they stood, alone, a little withdrawn, watching the families give last-minute advice to Fred and Sean. Both boys of great height, Ian red-haired, Graham fair, there hung around them a faint atmosphere of disdainful independence, more I think the product of a certain kind of schooling which had taught them not to show their feelings than a true indication of their actual attitude. Sean, the smallest of the three, had retired into a brooding silence from which at long intervals he managed a wan smile for his mother and his younger sister.

For everyone there was a certain relief when the barrier was opened and we could occupy ourselves with the tasks of finding seats, packing in luggage and checking last-minute instructions. Then, as the whistle blew and the engine gave a shuddering snort, far up the platform a figure was spied running and waving, panting with the effort to get to us before the carriage actually moved. All Ian and Graham's indifference fell away from them as they leant out and urged him on. This was the master who had been instrumental at school in encouraging them to volunteer, and the fact that he had made a journey of some difficulty to be there to see them off testified to his interest in their welfare. He arrived as the train began to move, and we all stood shouting and waving as the four heads gradually receded into the distance — destination Singapore.

They soon recovered their spirits, and once on board the tanker settled down for the long weeks at sea. For many volunteers there was a common initial experience.

35

I am just recovering from a bout of sea-sickness. The swell in the Bay of Biscay didn't affect me, but yesterday the land swell off Southern Arabia brought me to my knees. I think the worst hurt was probably to my pride and to my illusions of being a natural sailor.

But after recovering from this the world lay ahead. Fred found it a fascinating place.

It is amazing to me that the world is not so densely populated as one might think. Since we reached the coast of Spain we have seen miles and miles of uninhabited coast, and miles and miles of dry, dry land. Suez was a real eye-opener. There we were steaming through the canal in a modern luxury tanker with air-conditioning, iced water, good food, radio, swimming-pool, etc., and there, about two hundred yards away, were mud buildings with a woman in black and a donkey: it might have been a scene from the Bible.

And Sean wrote:

The crew have been very friendly right from the start and the only person with whom our relationships haven't been unspoilt is the chief engineer, who got very annoyed with us for walking on the deck above his cabin when we were very green in the first few days. Since then we have kept out of his way.

This particular tanker went only as far as Kuwait and there the volunteers had to change ships for another going on to Singapore. As the tanker fleet was not run for our convenience there was an element of uncertainty about all these arrangements. We had been warned beforehand that in the event of any sort of emergency a tanker might well have to be diverted at sea for a destination quite other than the one it started for, and indeed there had been a rumour two weeks after the boys had left that their ship had been turned back in mid-ocean and sent to South America! However this tale proved to be untrue, and the week spent at Kuwait before the second half of the journey began was an experience in itself. It was Graham who described something of the impact which it made on them all.

We have been living above ourselves since last Saturday when the ship docked at Mina, at somebody else's expense. The 'somebody else' is the Kuwait Oil Company whose guests we are, and we are being treated as if we were a deputation from the House of Lords, and naturally enough we are lapping it all up with, I think, for the most part, our tongues in our cheeks. To sit in the Guest House Restaurant and have Indian waiters silently serving us with THE most exquisite and expensive food is, I feel, a little out of place when considering what we are journeying to Sarawak for.

It is a land of violent contrast; vivid impressions will always remain with me of the honking horns of berserk cars; bazaars of European shops: decay and splendour: old men who sit about smoking their hookahs and young children, still untouched by the country's newly-found wealth, playing about in their dark skins and shouting 'Ullo boy' to any pink-skinned materialist in sight. I have never seen such pretty and uninhibited children in my life.

While some volunteers were enjoying their first taste of tropical heat there were others whose journey lay through quite different latitudes.

In the far south, lying off the very tip of South America, were the Falkland Islands, the government of which had put in an urgent request for teachers. It was interesting to find that of all the projects this one, in lands cold, tiny, cut off, was the most popular choice with a large number of young men. This was difficult to understand; these islands lacked all the glamour of the tropics and even, so it seemed, the interest of a population different in colour or in language. But somehow the magic of the Antarctic lay over them and those finally chosen for this assignment were faintly envied by their fellows.

They travelled out on a Falkland Islands Dependency Ship, or on one of the research ships taking out supplies and men to the scientific stations round the foot of the world. This in itself had an element of glamour, although the journey, involving many weeks of monotonous steaming through the great oceans, could be dull and irksome. The first two to make this voyage were Chris and Andrew, and it was Chris who wrote and described it to us.

SHIP'S CAPTAIN

After leaving Ushant behind, grey, barren and cold, our next sight of land was the mythical town of Las Palmas, on a still, starlit night, with its lights a shimmering haze in the distance: there was something of magnetic fascination in these lights! The island loomed dark above the low lights, dark and mysterious, with occasional twinkles from the heights, and the whole effect suggested some lost paradise. Perhaps it was as well we passed it by at night so as not to spoil the fantasy!

We picked up the Governor of St Helena at Ascension Island and sailed on, leaving it blue and mysterious behind a cloud of strange, crying seabirds. The next stop, St Helena, I found the most enchanting place. Long narrow boats, powered by outboard motors, conveyed us to the shore for one shilling where some hundreds of natives stood, or sat, on either side of the landing-stage and gazed in silence as we disembarked. We were then beseiged by a mass of taxi drivers all clamouring to take us round the island. However at the top of 'Jacob's Ladder' — a precipitous series of steps up a cliff, we engaged a taxi — very dilapidated — and set off down a narrow winding road for the 'round tour'. The island is one of steep-sided valleys and high peaks, some of the hills drop almost sheer into the valleys and the effect is most impressive. It was spring there and there were great fields of Easter lilies and many other brightly coloured flowers — all growing wild: it was wonderful.

Tristan da Cunha was an outstandingly impressive place. From a distance of twenty miles the 7,000-foot peak could be seen jutting aggressively through a bank of cloud. The peak was covered, in some places, with snow.

On arrival at the island the canvas-covered (wooden-framed) boats came out, (we struck, luckily, one of the calm days of the year) and we managed to get ashore for an hour. The village, situated at the foot of a 3,000-foot cliff, is composed of croft-like houses of brown stone — all very primitive and poor. The streets are grassy rides — interspread with rocks and intersected by streams. There are one hundred and sixty-eight inhabitants — only five families — and the stock is on the whole poor. The main industry is fishing — and some of the men earn money this way. Perhaps the most outstanding feature of the place is the atmosphere. It is one of solitude and peacefulness of an immeasurable depth — and one senses a feeling of the island's utter remoteness.

It is an odd sensation. We were rowed back to the ship in the dark and sailed for Montevideo — only to be directed, two days out, for South Georgia to pick up two ill men.

On the way south the weather became colder, the seas very stormy, and there were many icebergs about. Finally we sailed up a blue fjord surrounded by snow-covered mountains to a Norwegian Whaling Station on South Georgia. We were entertained to drinks, cakes, coffee and liqueurs. On the next afternoon I walked to visit a Lord of Elephant seal near by. These are fantastic creatures, huge and excessively hairy, although their 'barks', 'roars' or what-you-will are, at first, a little alarming, they are relatively harmless. I find them fascinating and watched them for a long time. The jealousy between the bulls — huge tooth-scarred beasts — over infringement of their harems is fantastic! Most, in fact all, the bulls are much scarred from numerous and savage fights.

Travelling free, by courtesy of somebody else, had however its disadvantages. The most important of these was the uncertainty of the date of departure. Many of the ships concerned were cargo boats with flexible schedules apt to be further elasticised by dock strikes or disputes.

We sailed on Tuesday and arrived at Newport late on Wednesday to pick up hundreds of tons of equipment for the R.A.F. at Aden, and also one race horse for Calcutta and two dog mascots for the Hampshire Regiment in Aden. Since then I have been learning how powerful dock unions are. On Thursday the labour gangs swarmed on board, found out that they had not got the minimum number required to 'work' the ship and returned home for the day. At the first sign of rain the gangs closed the hatches. They are only reluctantly going back to work at the moment because they are being paid 'wet' money: compensation for getting wet!

If, on the other hand, the transport was a passenger liner it was often not until the very last moment that the company knew whether they were likely to have any unclaimed accommodation. One July day the telephone rang.

'This is the P. and O. Steamship Company. We can give you eight free passages for the Far East on August 1st. Will you accept them?'

Would we accept them?! The Solomon Islands, at that time our furthest-flung customer, had asked for six volunteers. To get them there was very costly, and also complicated. Now to have presented to us a large number of free passages as far as Australia represented a gift of some hundreds of pounds. We accepted warmly.

'By the way they are first class accommodation because it is there that we are underbooked.'

So far so good, but there were certain difficulties involved. The volunteers were all still at school, and would be until a few days before this sailing. They had been warned some weeks before to be ready to move at any date after school term finished, but had they taken the warning seriously, and would their mothers be prepared to part with them almost as soon as they had received them for the summer holidays? Some frantic telephoning followed – to homes, to schools: to headmasters and parents: to the youngsters themselves, which resulted a week later in eight young men, five destined for the Solomon Islands, two for Sarawak and one for North Borneo, perching uneasily on every extra chair that could be crammed into our small sitting room, consuming cakes without much appetite and asking anxious questions about what awaited them.

They eyed each other also with some apprehension. These were the companions with whom they would be associated at close quarters for eight long weeks, and with one of whom, maybe, they might become friend or enemy in the year that lay ahead. They were still single, uncertain individuals and would not cohere into any sort of corporate body until they had been some days at sea. Months later John wrote:

I have now been on Choiseul for over three weeks and things have gone with such a rush that I cannot really believe it. The memory of being in your sitting-room and leaving a cold, dismal Tilbury on 1st August are now distant memories, overshadowed by four months of which every day has brought a new experience, something learned, a problem encountered and solved – and to think that I might have been in a cold, and no doubt draughty, solicitor's office!

That particular voyage was a luxury one, although the group organised themselves to entertain the children on board and look after some of the sports, but they were all glad to arrive in Australia

PAINTING LIFE BOATS IN THE TROPICS

and change to being deck passengers on the Chinese trading vessel which was to take them on the last lap of the journey.

For those who travelled with the Royal Navy, however, work began the moment the ship sailed. Tim and Bev, en route for British Honduras, were given a lift by the navy as far as Jamaica.

We sailed from Portsmouth Harbour early on Wednesday, September 13th. We were living in the junior mess deck with the youngest sailors on board. They proved to be quite an amusing bunch. All were younger than I. Their language was abominable. They used swear words in every sentence, so much so that the whole object of swearing lost its meaning. However they were helpful, friendly and generous. They live completely for the present; what happened yesterday and what may happen tomorrow means nothing to them. When they are not talking about themselves or anything that concerns themselves, they quickly lose interest.

Although we helped to paint the ship's deck and to keep our mess deck tidy our main work was of an educational nature. Sailors aspiring to promotion to the ranks of leading seaman or petty officer must pass a series of examinations; and while the ship is away at sea educational classes are run. We were introduced to the 'pupils' as qualified teachers, and it was explained that while we were aboard they should turn this golden opportunity available to their own advantage. Tim took charge of the English while I was landed with the Arithmetic. Progress was slow and laboured with most of the sailors.

After this experience facing the school class in British Honduras was not quite such an ordeal as it had once seemed it might be.

Although a fair proportion of the volunteers travelled in unorthodox ways a great number did, of course, go by the ordinary routes. All the girls, perhaps rather to their disappointment, did the journey by air. However, even going this way, there could be unforeseen incidents. It was Patrick, on the way to Bechuanaland, who had the most exciting plane journey.

I will not say that the trip was entirely without incident for, on the contrary, it was most exciting in parts! After ten minutes flying one of the four engines stopped and the pilot announced that he was going to jettison some fuel and return to Dusseldorf. This he did safely but, because of the nature of the trouble, a completely new aircraft was needed and we consequently had to wait two days before this was available.

All journeys however came to an end and as ships docked and planes touched down each volunteer had his first experience of the country in which he was to work for the next twelve months.

Fred and Sean had parted from Ian and Graham in Singapore and had gone on by air to Jesselton, the capital of North Borneo. Here they met the Director of Education and were told that they would go up country as teachers to a Chinese middle school.

This was a difficult assignment, and that they were not the first pair to tackle it made it, in some ways, more complicated, for they had also to contend with comparison with their predecessors.

North Borneo was, at this time, a small country at the northern tip of the island of Borneo, a British Colonial territory. Like most of the Borneo countries the greater part of its development lay around the coastline, although there was a single railway track, stretching up into the interior from the capital, along which lay small scattered townships. This was a very beautiful land, its coast fringed with blue South Sea islands, its interior crowned by Mount Kinabalu which rose over 13,000 feet into the air. The population was multiracial, consisting of Malay, Chinese, and the indigenous peoples of the interior including Dusun, Murut and Bajao. In this particular territory the problem of this multiracial community was one with which the volunteers were directly concerned; and it was in the schools, as teachers, that the Director of Education felt they could make a contribution.

Of the schools those which were purely Chinese, speaking this language and with a strong bias towards a Chinese culture, were the most challenging to work in. They were inward-turning, inclined to be a closed society with little contact with the rest of the community and no real commitment to the idea of North Borneo as a common homeland for both themselves and those of differing racial background. It was this attitude that it was hoped the volunteers might alter, even if only slightly, by being themselves outgoing and able, because of their youth, to take their contemporaries with them in the experience of discovery; but this was no easy task, as Fred and Sean had been warned in advance.

By the time they arrived in Jesselton, the capital, after six weeks at sea, they were ready to get down to any kind of job. Though enjoyable, the journey had passed slowly, and even once in North Borneo they were still not on their project.

At last, eight weeks after leaving Liverpool Street, we set off for Tenom. On arrival at the station we parked our luggage and went to get the tickets. However we were told the line was blocked and we could not go. So, resignedly, we put the bags back into the car and got in, ready for another few days wait. Just as we were leaving out came an official to say that the line was unblocked and we could go. So out came the suitcases again and we said 'goodbye' to both our host and to Jesselton.

We reached Tenom after an interesting nine-and-a-quarter-hour, eighty-seven-mile, journey. We shared our carriage with a bundle of live crabs, a live chicken in a basket, and young mothers who quite openly breast-fed their babies. I'm afraid this would be impossible in England, where there would be many stupid sniggers.

But although the end of the journey had been so eagerly looked forward to, there was a sense of flatness and uncertainty when it was actually accomplished. Tenom is a remote small town and all those immediately concerned with them were Chinese. There were only about half a dozen Europeans living in the vicinity, and at first there was a curious sensation of being somewhere completely strange, which was yet not the wild and primitive community that they had sometimes imagined.

Sean wrote shortly after they had arrived:

We welcome mail like manna from heaven. It isn't that I feel homesick here, but I like the contact with England. The train's arrival is one of the highspots of our day for we know that once it is in the mail will arrive in half an hour. We do not have the key to our school box, but we go to the post office and coax our letters from the postmaster whom we are friendly with.

In the next door territory of Sarawak, Graham went up-river to a totally different kind of project. This was a community development scheme which had been one of the original consumers of volunteers. Situated in Sea Dayak, or Iban, country, it was reached not by road or rail but by river. It was one of Graham's predecessors who wrote:

I should call this journey from Kuching, the capital, the first really unusual experience we had. This voyage down a tropical river was so completely different. Even Kuching had, in many ways, been very ordinary to us and was a town in which one quickly felt at home. However, now one was in the wild and for the first time we saw a Malay kampong (village) in the flesh. I was conscious of the silence of the sago palms along the river, and I realised how utterly remote all these places were, with water as their chief lines of communication and transport. It was an overcast day and certainly there was little glamour in this part of the tropics, I thought.

That night, after entering the Krian River we spent the night at Kabong, the kampong with the Chinese bazaar where nearly all ships stop before proceeding to Saratok. Communication with our crew was difficult because we did not know a word of Chinese. However, we finally ascertained that we would not be travelling further that night, and struggled ashore through the mud and over the elaborate gangplanks of bamboo, etc. This really was an experience, especially as we were still keen to keep our new shoes clean. How much we had to learn! We wandered round the village and its smells, all I think, feeling a little lost. I do not like Kabong even now.

How different up in the 'ulu'. The following morning saw a different picture and we were all pleased to arrive at Saratok in bright sunshine. Two Dayak boys had been sent down with a canoe specially to meet us. They looked after us well. We bought more kit and essentials, as directed by the boys, in the bazaar, and after various hospitalities and a meeting with the District Officer we proceeded up-river in a government boat, the canoe following after overflowing with our baggage.

The very last stage of this same journey into the 'ulu' the headwaters of a river, could be made on foot or in a canoe. The whole expedition would have taken two or perhaps three, days and most volunteers were glad to arrive by this time.

My behind was getting used to sitting in boats and my skin was covered in bites, so it was no great hardship to clamber into a canoe for the final stages.

Not every journey ended in such an unsophisticated manner or in such remote surroundings. The projects were as varied in their own way as were the boys, and one of the fascinating aspects of the scheme was fitting the two together and then taking infinite trouble to ensure that each

MALAY MAN

boy went to his assignment not only excited by the challenge in front of him but also convinced that this was his particular niche for which he was peculiarly fitted. It was this care and effort that contributed, in a large measure, to the very small rate of failure in the first years.

Douglas, who went to Nyasaland, was a boy of cheerful, faintly sardonic temperament, articulate and intelligent, ready to ride over difficulties. He knew, as did all those going to Central Africa, that there were likely to be very delicate situations arising requiring all a volunteer's common sense and self-control. At this time Nyasaland was engaged in a bitter political struggle to establish the leadership of Dr Banda and extricate herself from the Federation, and, as in all the under-developed countries, students formed one of the most active political groups. Douglas, going out to teach in the one government secondary school with a sixth form in the whole country, was well aware that the question of loyalties would not be a straightforward one.

He and another volunteer travelled out by ship to South Africa and then had to take the train up to Nyasaland.

Richard and I had a most pleasant journey up, though there were extreme complications over ticket bookings at Port Elizabeth. We docked on Thursday, September 22nd at 6 a.m., and just caught the train at 2.30 p.m. the same day—though owing to the time factor this meant abandoning half our luggage on the station. We do not expect to see it again. The train takes five days and four nights, and goes through Kimberley, Mafeking, Bulawayo, Salisbury and Dondo Junction, at the last three of which you have to change. It arrived at Limbe at officially seven o'clock in the evening of Monday, September 26th.

Owing to unforeseen circumstances, to wit, a train delay, we were unable to contact the Education Department at Zomba before, but when we did so we were promptly met, were interviewed by, and had lunch with everybody who matters there. After two nights I flew up to Lilongwe. I reached the school in the evening, and was promptly inveigled into a staff poetry club meeting, which gives you a good idea of the staff here. They are very much alive, play basketball and cricket, and do Scottish dancing.

I never envisaged for a moment that I should write this letter while listening to a record of *Così fan Tutte* after a superb lunch

46

served with absolutely correct ritual in a house whose walls are lined with most expensive and excellent books.

The luggage, after some vicissitudes, turned up a few weeks later, by which time Douglas had moved on from the comparatively simple staff relationships with his own compatriots to the much more complex friendships with his pupils.

On the whole living arrangements were fairly simple, and again there was no set rule; each project made the arrangements which suited it best. Sometimes the volunteer stayed with a kindly-disposed government officer, sometimes he lived in the school — occasionally even he slept in a dormitory with the boys, sometimes he lived on his own finding out as best he could, and with the help of a local servant, how the mysteries of housekeeping worked. Very few volunteers were concerned with the actual mechanics of how they lived, and information on this subject was usually the result of a direct request. In the Gambia for instance:

The college buildings, sleeping quarters, assembly hall and schoolrooms are those used by chickens and farm managers from the days of the great Egg Scheme. It sounds very primitive, but the houses are all stone-built and watertight, and we have one house to ourselves. This has a bedroom, a small storeroom and a refrigerator room (with a large frig) and a sitting-room with several 'easy' chairs and tables, etc. We have the same dinner of rice and bony gristly meat as do the students, and we cook our own evening meal from tinned stuff provided.

Very quickly these strange domestic surroundings became normal, and the volunteer began to look outward, to assess the people among whom he was to work and live.

Peter and David were the first two volunteers ever to go to Somaliland, at that time a British Colonial territory, but within their year to become independent and leave the Commonwealth. They were to go as teachers, but the request had also stated that they wished for a boy who could give a boost to Scouting in the territory. Peter was a Queen's Scout from the north of England, a gentle, kind boy with an impish circular haircut. His companion, David, came from the south-west, dark and quiet. These two, who were to pioneer in a very real sense, struck up a warm friendship which not only supported them during the crises of their year, but lasted long after it.

They were, in many ways, very cut off. Somaliland was a Moslem country, small, hot, largely desert. We had few contacts there and were not able to give much guidance other than of a general kind. The role of a volunteer overseas was completely strange to this part of the world at this time, and Peter and David had the responsibility of creating it. Neither had been much out of Britain before.

Shortly after they arrived they wrote:

We have both been impressed by the high intelligence and open-mindedness of the educated adults and the eagerness of the pupils to learn. However, it is inevitable that we shall learn more than we shall teach. On the first day of term a boy came to the Trades School to ask if there was a vacancy. On being told that there wasn't he was nearly in tears.

Teachers and town elders seem most impressed and grateful to our status as volunteers. These are first impressions which may, however, be changed or subdued by future contact with the Somali people of the interior.

Something of the feelings of a volunteer on the day when he first faced his job, after the months or weeks of imagining, dreaming, travelling, were expressed by Chris writing about his own arrival in the Falkland Islands. It is true that the surroundings were unique and very different from that of any other single volunteer. The Falklands teacher had a widely scattered beat to travel. His children lived in remote farmsteads on the many islands that composed the group and it was the job of the teacher to work his way round, staying a while with each family, teaching the children, helping the parents, and then setting homework to be done while he moved on to the next farm. This was a pattern followed nowhere else, but Chris's description contains also the sense of uncertainty, nostalgia and loneliness that leapt out at most volunteers when they first realised that they were faced with the reality of their commitment.

The Beaver seaplane will land him in the small bay: a boat will pull out from the jetty and come alongside the floats of the Beaver: his luggage will be unloaded into the boat, the door of the plane will slam, and while he is being rowed to the jetty the plane will take off and he will watch the last link with civilisation become a dot and then disappear. There will be no introductions, and as he walks past the wool shed up to the single house he will experience the odd sensation that he is on his own, surrounded by water, a hundred miles from the only town—and among completely strange people.

TUG

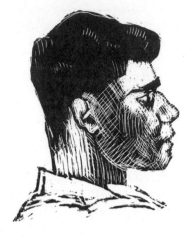

GARETH

Teaching

As soon as requests for help began to come in spontaneously from countries overseas we found that schools formed a high percentage of our customers. At first we were chary of sending volunteers out to teach. There seemed valid arguments against it and, on our side, we felt that to send young men straight from school back to school might be both dull and unadventurous.

However it quickly became obvious that the flood of requests for teachers, which continued to come in, represented a real need. So urgent was the staffing situation in many schools that the choice lay not between a volunteer or a professional, between an expatriate helper or a local boy, but between one of our youngsters or nobody. We had also learned on the early experimental projects that school-leavers could teach – and teach well.

The deciding factor in the acceptance of teaching projects was the realisation that the school overseas, far from being a dull project, did in fact provide an admirable situation for a volunteer. It gave him a stable background in which to work and a recognised job to do, both important to his being able to make the fullest use of his time and his gifts. The school also provided a community, the pupils and teachers, in which he could gain acceptance and through which he could enter the wider life of the village, the district, the country. It was important, however, that both sides recognised that this reaching out from the school and taking its pupils with him was an integral part of the volunteer's job, and the one aspect of it in which his youth was his real qualification and his great asset. We could see, at our end, that the volunteer understood this, but we had also, in so far as was possible, to select the schools that would give him this scope and opportunity.

As far as the volunteer was concerned he was offered no choice of project. It was left to us, as indeed it had to be, to make the decision as to where the talents and aptitudes of any one individual could best be used; and we took a great deal of care to place each youngster, in so far as was possible, in the kind of situation which would use all of him to the maximum. Inevitably, however, this meant that some volunteers, who had imagined themselves working with remote and primitive peoples in jungle conditions, were disappointed at the prospect of the reality — a new secondary school in a town. It was very important that they should be enabled to see that the challenge in this kind of project was equally great. Just as each volunteer had his or her individual talents which it must be our concern to see used to the full, so each project had its own special importance — or we did not accept it as a project — and this had to be analysed and made plain to the volunteer. It was a measure of our sucess in this difficult exercise that we hardly ever had a volunteer who wished that he had gone to a different job.

Schools varied enormously, not only from one part of the world to another but even within one territory. There were government schools, often well housed and equipped, dealing with an intelligent and sophisticated elite, sometimes less physically well-off but struggling to raise the whole standard of education in a country; there were mission schools, usually poor, often very remote, without whom in some cases there would be no sort of education at all, not always certain whether their battle was against ignorance or against secular competition; there were independent schools, schools run by a company primarily for the benefit of its employers, schools which had sprung into being ad hoc because of the tremendous thirst for learning among the children.

We drew no ideological lines when it came to supplying a volunteer. Our criteria were simple and fundamental: was there really a worthwhile job to be done, and would the volunteer be fully used, overworked if necessary? The great danger in sending these young men overseas was not mental or physical strain, it was boredom. The one situation that the volunteers could not cope with was to arrive and find that they were not really needed. Heat, frustration inadequate living, hostility, unhappiness, all these could be overcome if there was a job to be done; without the job everything else collapsed. For this reason we went to infinite trouble to ensure that the work was real and essential. For this reason, also, it was made plain to the volunteer that his work did not stop at the classroom door; he was on the job twenty-four hours a day, seven days a week, twelve months in the year, and he was encouraged to use the whole gamut of his talents and skills and hobbies, and to take others with him while doing so.

In North Borneo there was some difficulty in establishing a channel of communication between pupil and teacher. This was especially so in schools where the majority of students were of Chinese origin, and both a strong sense of racial pride and an ingrained respect for 'face' made the first few weeks a battle in which the volunteer was fighting not only his own fears and weaknesses but also the resistance of his pupils. The lad teaching a mixed racial class at a mission school, in a small coastal town described this situation.

I remember someone telling me that the pupil-teacher relationship was impossible to overcome' with primary schoolchildren (who, by the way, are often as old as their counterparts in the secondary schools). I've only been teaching five days but I think he was overstating things slightly. There are difficulties. Most of them can be overcome, though.

These are what I have judged to be the main problems in this country where 'face' is so important, the girls and boys very loath to commit themselves. With this goes a natural shyness, I think, which combines with the former to give the teacher the impression that they understand thoroughly things about which they have not a clue. For instance on Wednesday I was doing collectives in English — a 'flock' of sheep, etc. I spent about five minutes trying to coax out of anyone the collective for wolves; when I suddenly realised — they can't know what a wolf is. I asked them. Sure enough, and slowly enough, (they can't even put up their hands unless someone will do it with them) they admitted this.

I ask a boy if he understands. He will not seem to realise that I want the truth but just says what he thinks I want him to say. Even

VILLAGE SCHOOL, WEST AFRICA

so it is hard to get really exasperated. These children are mostly so willing. I try to bring them into the lesson as much as I can, both physically and mentally. Instead of all bookwork where a boy or girl feels relatively 'safe' to work quietly away, a girl comes out to the blackboard and shows the class, or a boy tells another boy how a thing is done. Even in five days this has had results. I am beginning to get slight impudence from the cocky ones in a class. I count this as progress and do not stamp it down too much.

Inland, in the Chinese middle school at Tenom, Fred and Sean too had their problems. Shortly after arriving Fred wrote:

I began teaching full of beans and oozing with confidence. I found I could make the children laugh, and was happy that I could do so. However, things began to degenerate and reached an all-time low last week, when I was feeling very depressed. It all started with a notice being pinned on my back by one of the junior forms. It was in Chinese. I discovered the culprit and harangued him. I later discovered that it said 'a friend' which lifted my gloom a little. However I have now made it clear to them that I will stand no nonsense, and it is now my most co-operative and happy form.

The other form I had difficulty with was Senior 1 (the slower seniors). They seemed to think that they could tell me what to do, and I am now in process of making it clear to them that in the classroom I am in complete control. 'I shall succeed,' I say, gritting my teeth every time I walk in to teach them. However this time alone will tell.

Thus I started off over-confidently, degenerated to complete shakiness, and have now achieved the happy state of confident apprehensiveness.

Up until very recently the medium of instruction in this school had been Chinese and most of the pupils and staff came from this racial background. In a sense this had meant that they were to some extent cut off from the rest of their fellow citizens, cocooned within a language and a culture which it was difficult for them to break out of or any non-Chinese to break into. Now the medium of instruction was to be changed to English which, along with Malay, was a common language for the territory, and this change, while

54

making things very difficult within the school gave added importance to the presence of the volunteers – the only members of staff whose mother tongue it was. Sean described some of the practical problems involved.

In the teaching line we have come to the school in the first year that they have started to do all their lessons in English. This means that Fred has to teach biology and geography and I have to teach English grammar as well as conversation, reading and essay writing. The standard of English is very low indeed, and it is all they can do to understand the readers we had last term which were almost kindergarten standard. The English books they have this year are, at my most conservative estimate, about two years too far advanced for them, and I think it is nearer three. I started the new book with one form yesterday and spent the whole of the forty-minute lesson going through the introduction to the piece they were reading. It was only nine lines long!

I don't mind this as it is a challenge to be teaching under these conditions.

A year later the problem was still there, but it was slowly beginning to be overcome. Hugh, who succeeded Sean, described his efforts to conquer the same problems. Both he and Sean suffered many moments of depression when they felt that little or no progress was being made, and wondered whether it had been worthwhile attaching them to the school at all. But to those outside it was plain that, very slowly, a change was coming over the atmosphere in the school and that, in the matter of English alone, there was a much greater willingness to try to speak it than there had been before.

Their English is slowly improving. You have to try and take their pronunciation to bits and start all over again teaching them sounds. Then you find they read a sentence word by word, because they learn the words originally by saying them over and over again separately, so that each sentence becomes a string of widely separated words, each word, however, said quickly and sharply. They do not raise or lower the voice in a sentence at all. All this does not matter with those who will never learn English anyway, but it is a real handicap for the more intelligent ones who will continue their education.

When it comes to teaching something where a bit of elementary thought is all that is required, such as punctuation or grammar, immediately the lack of grammar and punctuation in their own language makes it very difficult for them. I have experimented with using their own tried method of learning by heart, hoping that making general association of inverted commas with spoken sentences, etc., they will learn that way. On the whole I enjoy teaching and the problems it brings immensely, though I am keenly aware of my inexperience and ignorance of teaching methods.

In the neighbouring territory of Sarawak, Ian, working in a government secondary school with a multiracial student population, found his pupils easy to get on with but had difficulty with his own nervousness. A boy of fine physical presence, red-haired and very tall, he was nevertheless diffident about his own abilities, and the aloof independence he had shown at Liverpool Street station when we saw him off by no means mirrored the reality. He had had certain qualms about his posting because he felt that he would be conspicuous by his height in a country where most people were fairly small, and it took him some time to overcome his initial fears.

The day I took over I only had two periods which actually went off fairly well. It was the apprehension beforehand which got me down and when, in my preparations, I burnt my hand on some hot glass, I felt more like packing up and going home than I have ever done since I left England. I have been given the option of further periods if I want them, and I hope to take up the offer when I get into the swing of things a bit more and when my classroom manner improves. At the moment I tend to gabble and leave rather important points out in the momentum of speech.

He did eventually take up the option on the extra classes and not so long afterwards he was teaching, without any apparent effort, a great many periods of science, algebra and English. He also taught

... one period of general knowledge. I have only taken this period once and when I asked what they wanted to talk about I was met by the concerted voice of thirty-six Dayaks, Kayans, Kenyahs, Malays and Melanus, shouting 'England'. I thought a talk on the situation in the U.N.O. would be more educational, but I soon capitulated and the end of the period found me demonstrating how to hold a cricket bat with the blackboard ruler.

A number of the Sarawak volunteers went into schools run by the Anglican mission. These schools suffered severely from a lack of adequate staff and volunteers serving in them found themselves responsible for a varied number of duties. They also, very often, felt that the existing facilities were very inadequate and set about to rectify the situation. Christopher's description of his normal day-to-day job gives a fair picture of the heavy burden of responsibility which volunteers could find themselves carrying.

The school was a boarding one serving a large area up one of the big rivers and the Dayak boys would come down from their long-houses by canoe. A part of the function of the school was to instruct and set an example in hygiene, simple agriculture and other skills which the boys could take back to their houses, and one of the big problems of increasing standards of academic education was the finding of a right balance between these two aspects of the curriculum.

I have had a very eventful term and am utterly exhausted. I have been appointed boarding-house master and consequently have responsibility for 160 boarders. I have never had so much work to do before. I am doing full-time teaching, Form Three mostly as we are unable to get a permanent teacher.

My duties as boarding master are very varied—anything from catering to curing minor ills to collecting fees and seeing parents, to inspecting dormitories and trying to prevent them from further decay, and if possible improve them. We are putting more emphasis now on outdoor work. The boarding-houses have started a big market gardening effort, but they do need pushing all the time to plant things and make experiments with manure and soils. I am becoming quite a farmer. We are going to turn a good bit of our swamp over to rice in the summer. We have started rearing chickens, and except for a nasty moment when they nearly got fowl pest and I had to inject sixty on a Saturday morning, they have supplied us with some good chicken curries.

I have built a fish pond which now supports fifteen fish, and a pig pen on top. We have been hacking down secondary jungle around the compound (and have found thirty snakes), felled a lot of trees and then burned the debris ready for rubber, pineapples and maize. The lack of water on the compound is a great problem. There were no decent bathing pools previously and not much drinking water, in fact the school had to adjourn sometimes in summer through lack of water. I have sunk two new wells and built a couple of swimming pools. This next term I hope we shall be able to build a second fish pond and a new playing field and a new dormitory.

This pattern was not an unusual one in parts of the world other than Sarawak. In fact one of the great advantages of sending such young volunteers was their ability to adapt themselves, quickly and easily, to a life which demanded a multiplicity of general skills rather than one or two specialisations. And where the older man, out for a longer period, might have felt it necessary to conserve something of his energies the youngster, on the job only for a year, was prepared not only to do everything that was asked of him but also to spend what free time he had on extra activities.

I told the seniors that they could come to the house with any questions or problems they might have, and since then we have been besieged by as many as ten at any one time waiting their turn in the queue. They have appeared before breakfast and late at night with their inexhaustible supply of questions, some of which are so elementary that one wonders just what they have been taught in nine years at school, and by the time night falls we are just about all in.

That was Keith. David, who shared the house with him and worked in the same school, had strong views on some of the educational ideas which he was encountering. When this happened, as it did not infrequently, the volunteer had to tread delicately. He needed not only a sense of responsibility but a clear idea of his own place in the overall pattern of work overseas if he was to make a satisfactory and worthwhile contribution without antagonising those with whom he worked. Most volunteers behaved admirably in the really difficult situations and this was due I think, in large measure to their knowledge that we had complete confidence in them to do so and in their freedom to discuss with us, at long distance, the problems which troubled them.

We have just got over a spate of marking from the exams and I was fairly pleasantly surprised by some of the results we obtained. There is an appalling idea rampant here of a 50% pass or fail mark which, besides being absurdly out of date, is hideously discouraging for the boys and girls themselves. I am sure that if that principle could be obliterated we would do away with large numbers of pupils who ask to leave because 'they failed their exams'. My educational theory is based entirely on personal experience at the receiving end, but I know that I was always taught to use the internal examinations as a pointer for the effort required in the next term or year. Here I have heard no mention of that idea. Surely with an emotional race such as the Dayaks encouragement and not discouragement is the correct approach?

The teaching, however, was not all on one side, and both parties to the arrangement recognised this. After he had been in Sarawak for some months Geoff wrote:

> I wish that I were more skilled in carpentry, etc. Although I've done a little it in no way matches up with the carpentry I'm doing now. I think my work in the field is best summed up by one of the boys who, after we'd worked together for about two months on and off, said rather hesitatingly, 'Sir, you have learnt quite a lot since we began!' I agreed.

The kind of job to be done in schools did not differ very much in the Solomon Islands. But for the volunteers there the big disillusion was the lack of glamour. I suppose that for most of us the Solomon Islands and their location, the Pacific Ocean, conjured up pictures of sunny South Sea islands inhabited by extremely beautiful and happy people. The reality was very different.

Niven was one of the first two volunteers ever to go to the Solomon Islands and, at that time, we were not even very sure of their exact location or how best to get there. The R.A.F. had offered a lift as far as Singapore, and after that, because of the infinite complications involved in booking a seat from an intermediate stopping place, the boys would have to make the arrangements themselves. They were given an adequate supply of money, an introduction in Singapore with whom to stay, and as much useful information as could be mustered in London — on the whole remarkably little — about air connections to Pacific Islands.

Niven was a Catholic, a boy whose skills lay in his hands, good at carpentry and hoping eventually to be an art student. A request had come in from a Catholic mission in the Solomons for a boy who would help in the school and be a general handyman on one of their out-stations, and we chose Niven. He was a quiet boy for whom this was a tremendous step, and as the moment drew nearer and nearer when he would travel down to an airfield somewhere in England and take off into the unknown he grew even quieter and paler that he had been before.

The journey was not a simple one, and it proved almost as complicated to board a long-distance aeroplane in mid-route at Singapore when one was on the spot as it had appeared to be when we tried it from London. However they did eventually arrive safely, and with more confidence than they had started out. For us it was a curious sensation to open Niven's first letter and find that it came from Guadalcanal, a name with vivid war-time associations which seemed quite unrelated to our present preoccupations.

The school, of some sixty pupils, is held in a native house which also serves as our house and the dispensary. Standards can hardly be attached to the academic qualities of our pupils, for many of them have, until recently, been living in the bush: therefore they lack even the ability to speak pidgin English.

School here does not, therefore, occupy the majority of our time. The Marau district is, unhappily, one of much sickness, not so much malaria or polio, but diseases of the skin especially leprosy and bakwa, caused purely through the dirty conditions under which they live. So almost every day there is a batch of bodies (metaphorically speaking) to be daubed with lotion and ointment. I expect there will be quite an amount of building to be done here, but as yet the materials have not arrived; when they do, however, I hope to lend a hand to production.

As in Sarawak, schools could vary tremendously, and the staffing position was often desperate.

The High School has one class of thirteen boys, whose ages range from eighteen to twenty-two and one teacher—myself. I am in almost sole charge of the school and my classroom is a rapidly disintegrating and decomposing native hut.

So wrote one of the Solomon Islands volunteers, and the indignation that grew out of experiences like this was later to carry many of them back to their own country with a heightened sensitivity to under-privilege everywhere and a determination not to be satisfied until they had qualified themselves to do something about it.

In Malaya Michael found himself in a somewhat different situation. The request which he went out to fulfil had come from an orphanage run by a well-known charitable society. It was housed in

60

FAR EAST PUPIL

a poor district of Penang, and took boys, mostly of Chinese origin, who were destitute or homeless. As so often with endeavours of this kind the needs had grown and expanded quite regardless of staffing problems or financial difficulties. It had been found expedient to add a school to the Home to cater for the children who could not get into other schools, and to help with finances pupils, whose parents paid a small sum towards their education, were taken from the surrounding community.

When Michael was allotted to this project it had been understood that his work would lie mainly in the Home, and that help in the school would be largely in extra activities. He was well suited to this being a boy of gentle, kindly nature, anxious to do his best but of no great academic distinction.

However, between the time of his allocation and his actual arrival on the spot considerable staff changes had taken place in the Home, and he and his companion volunteer, a young carpenter prepared to teach his own trade, found themselves arriving in a hiatus in staff affairs which eventually meant that they were more experienced in working overseas by some weeks than the superintendent who was their superior. Michael, a good grammar school education his model in a difficult situation, rose to meet the problems admirably.

I understood that I was to specialise in gymnastics, but shortly after my arrival I learnt that I had been made the headmaster of this school, consisting of six primary classes and one secondary class. I begin work at 8.30 a.m. in the office, doing accounts, discussing problems with the staff and putting forward propositions, checking supplies and whether or not we can afford them. At 12.30 p.m. I start teaching our one secondary class until 6 p.m., when I snatch tea and begin marking books. I must confess that much of my work has been bluff for these last weeks, e.g. teaching Chinese History and Tropical Health.

Apart from the school I have further responsibilities in the

Home. The children here range from seven years to twenty-three, and many have totally different backgrounds, and many of their habits are hard to stamp out. I am thinking particularily of gambling which seems to be our main concern. Some children are illegitimate, some out of control, some simply deserted by their parents, and when friction occurs between the boys these factors have to be taken into consideration. Straight from school to head-master is really quite a shock and it makes one wonder who is on the receiving end the student or the master. However it has given me a great sense of responsibility and I feel I cannot let these people down.

Later on, still in the throes of an exacting job not made easier by his own sense of indignation at some of the values he was dealing with, or by the fact that he and his companion lived a life of austerity and extremely hard work in the midst of a sophisticated and very beautiful city, he wrote:

The new school year started with a bang on the morning of January 2nd. My office was packed with parents wanting to register their children, teachers and students clamouring for books and other requirements, whilst boys and girls were running in and out getting in everyone's way. This went on for three days and I never had breakfast until about 10.30 a.m. How I kept a level head I don't know. I gave out some five hundred exercise books and then we ran out of stock. The staff were getting impatient with me and I was getting impatient with the printers. However, after ten days things began to run smoothly and then one of the teachers had to leave us to deliver her baby and I had to teach both in the morning and the afternoon and do my office work at night. No sooner had the term started than the Education Department started to send piles of forms along.

It is perhaps surprising after this to learn that Michael changed his plans for his future and decided to train as a teacher!

The situation was very different in the Falkland Islands. Here the small number of pupils (perhaps six or seven to each volunteer) and the scattered nature of the farms meant that the volunteer worked wholly on his own without the framework of a school or the fellow-ship of other teachers to help him. He was 'the teacher', watched for by the children as he travelled on horseback from one farm to the next, welcomed by the parents, as much for his assistance in the everyday matters of the farm and the news he might bring with him as for the education he brought their children. But what he taught and how he taught it, and his responsibility towards his office were entirely a matter for his own conscience. Chris expressed something of this when he wrote:

I find that the main difficulty living on these islands is setting standards and keeping them, for it is only too easy to let both work and tongue relapse in this lazy isolation. The secondary difficulty is persuading parents of the importance of education (the *meaning* of the word) and the fact that homework must be done.

Homework was one of the problems. It was not just a matter of setting it one evening and correcting the next day. On the contrary the teacher might be away for a number of weeks, during which the children had to have adequate and properly graded work to do on their own. The only help available to them if they came across difficulties was that of their parents and this meant that Chris had to explain as far as he could to the mother and father exactly what it was he wanted the children to do. No easy task.

I am in the middle of setting ten weeks homework to the three children here—and it has to be comprehensible to the parents as well! So you can see that I do work.

This was written in reply to a comment on letters from both Chris and Andrew which had dwelt at some length on the extra curricular activities which occupied a considerable amount of their time. It was important, both for their own happiness and for their acceptability by the farm families, that they should be able to enter fully into the normal preoccupations of their hosts. Andrew described some of these.

The day begins at six. Shearing has just finished and dipping has now started. When shearing was in progress I helped till breakfast, school lasted from nine till three. After school, till five-thirty, I was again in the shearing shed. I am not a quick shearer (at first a sheep took me three quarters of an hour), but by the end I had begun to get the knack. We have supper at seven-thirty, after knocking off time till supper I have been painting the settlement motor-boat. After supper we talk, listen to the wireless and go early to bed. At the weekends I usually go fishing or shooting geese. The geese are the pest of the Falklands since they eat the grass, but are very good to eat.

Such was the success of Chris and Andrew in this work, work for which it had been found almost impossible to recruit trained teachers, that at the end of the year replacements were asked for and negotiations entered into for sending a greater number. When Chris and Andrew boarded the ship at Port Stanley to leave for England they found awaiting them telegrams of good wishes from every island in the group on which they had taught.

By a curious chance their successors both had the same Christian name—Robert, and they looked not unalike physically being both tall, fair boys with pink outdoor complexions. To differentiate them we called one Rob and the other Bob, though even this had its hazards as it was not always easy to remember which was which.

Due to the difficulties of shipping arrangements there was a considerable gap in the time between Chris and Andrew's departure and the arrival of the Roberts. As always when the first volunteers had been a success we were nervous for those who followed. It was not always easy to live up to predecessors who had scored a hit, and employers, too, could be difficult in expecting an exact replica of their first boys! We need not, however, have worried in this instance. Though less articulate the Roberts were equally welcome and responsible.

Rob described in a letter what he found on arrival.

When I did get out here, however, I found three charming well-brought up children, anxious to start school having had none since Andrew left in August. Because my pupils are willing I get on well in school and none of them appear to be backward or lazy.

Later on some of the problems came to light and he wrote:

I am getting on well with my pupils and most of them have improved during the last six months ... I now have a shepherd's home to visit, two hours ride from here, where I have three pupils. Two I shall have to start from scratch and the third, who is eleven, has only had three months schooling. I have just sent in for books which will come out when the next boat comes round this way. My thirteen-year-old pupil has come on very well and could have won a scholarship to Dorset last year. Unfortunately she is not interested, and wants to be a maid at the manager's

THE JOB

house. She is teaching herself shorthand and is a good mathematician. I am going to start teaching her French, which she is keen to learn.

Teaching all over the world was not without its lighter moments, and some unorthodox subjects were taught and curious questions answered. Douglas, in Nyasaland, reported that

> In the course of my ordinary teaching I have taught one form to read music, three to recognise the Russian alphabet, and two some Roman history. This is all officially General Science, but there's nothing like a liberal education, especially after exams!

He also invented ways of keeping his pupils interested.

> My teaching methods are becoming progressively more dubious as the term goes on. I have now resorted to political propaganda to keep my General Scientists interested. For instance, in order to demonstrate the properties of chlorine I tore out the line 'Vote for Kamuzu' (Dr Banda) from a party leaflet and blotted it out with ink. During the lesson I bleached the ink, leaving the print still legible. Cries of 'Long Live Mr R.' 'You are Malawi, Sir,' etc. I think they might remember that one.

Peter, too, in Somaliland, found that science embraced a wide horizon and could bring up complex issues!

> My main subject at the moment is science and it presents some delightful questions and incidents, and I am afraid some of the answers I have to give to make things comprehensible to the pupils would not be looked on very favourably in scientific circles.
> 'Do you know how the air gets into a ship to make it float?' 'Is it true that the government pay teddy-boys to go round beating up old people?' 'You know London, have you ever seen the Prime Minister in Soho coffee bars paying off "the gang", or queues of teddy-boys around Downing Street?' Such are the questions and some are not so easy to answer or explain, but we try our best.

It is easy to smile at naivety, but such queries do reveal in their own way the enormous gulf of political misunderstanding which can exist on both sides between countries, and it may be that it was only

65

answers by boys which could convince other boys that they were being told the truth. Any adult answering if indeed he had taken the trouble, might well have found himself viewed with deep suspicion as a government agent and therefore automatically untrustworthy.

In 1961, as a direct result of a visit made earlier by my husband to Saigon, a request came from Vietnam for a volunteer to help with the teaching of English in the University of Hué, and to assist also with Scouting. This was an exciting possibility; it was one of the few applications at this time from a country quite outside the British sphere of influence, and we were anxious to accept the project if we could.

There were strong feelings among those concerned both for and against sending a young man out on his own to a country so remote, and moreover one which was continuously engaged in a guerilla civil war with the Communists. On the one side it was felt that the risks were far too great and that to move out of the comfortable background of countries which had a historic connection with Britain was to expose a volunteer to immense hazards. On the other hand were those, among them ourselves, who felt that for Vietnam to ask for a young British volunteer was a gesture which should not be lightly disregarded. Experience also indicated that the really dangerous situations for volunteers lay not in countries with a 'foreign' background, but in the much subtler and more corrupting influences which could confront a youngster in countries of racial tension such as Kenya or Rhodesia. We were certain that the Vietnamese having asked for a volunteer, and being well aware that they were getting an eighteen-year-old, would feel all the anxious responsibility for him of a good host—and this, in fact, proved to be the case.

The only person who accepted without hesitation or reservation the decision that he should go to Vietnam was the volunteer himself; and his parents, having taken the momentous step of agreeing that John should volunteer at all, then gave him their complete confidence.

He was a Catholic boy, a Queen's Scout, and he spoke very adequate French. These three attributes, combined with integrity and strength of character, made him the obvious choice for a country which had a large Catholic section and where the lingua franca was French. In Hué, a walled university city in the north of the country very close to the line of fighting, he found himself the only Englishman—with consequent advantages.

BILL TEACHING

The fact that I am English, in contrast to American, is having a marked effect. It is quite astonishing the number of people who have spoken to me and asked me to give them private lessons, because they want to learn English and not 'American'.

However the overwhelming desire to learn English could have its disadvantages. He was in enormous demand to teach it, and gradually found himself not only with classes all day but in the evenings also. Even the Scouts felt that his value as a teacher was greater than his worth as a Scouter, rather to John's distress.

The Scoutmaster, who seems to have taken me under his wing, is very insistent that I give his Rovers English lessons, even at the expense of doing Scouting. I tried in the nicest possible way to explain, 1) that there was every opportunity in Hué for them to learn English elsewhere: 2) that I myself would be a little weary of English teaching and would not give my best, and 3) I want to help Scouting. I think I have managed to reach a compromise and for a start I am going to meet about seven or eight Rovers and instruct them in knotting, map interpretation, etc., giving them the English terms and letting them practice their English while asking.

His isolation, which had seemed a risk, proved to be the opposite. As with so many single volunteers he was forced from the very beginning to make his friends among those with whom he lived and worked, and they on their side, because they were aware of his possible loneliness, hastened to offer him friendship, glad I have no doubt in many instances that, for once, they could offer help to an Englishman.

The celebrations of Christmas and New Year have just come to a close, I regret to say, and I can say without any hesitation whatsoever that this festival has been the happiest of my life. I was lucky enough to receive invitations from all kinds of people, and I have experienced the festivity of Christmas not only with Americans and Vietnamese, but also with the Germans, Danes, French and Chinese.

And later on another festival.

Last week saw the most important festival of the Vietnamese year. It was Tet, or the Oriental New Year. One of the most pleasant customs for me was that of visiting. During the three days of Tet everyone pays a visit to his friends, relations and superiors. For me Tet lasted a whole week. I was invited by so many people to visit their homes that it would have been impossible to fit these visits into three days. I had a most enjoyable time and met most of the students' families.

He was a success. Although there had been no question of it in the original arrangement the University insisted on paying him a salary and, after consultation, it was agreed that he should accept this and use it for travelling during the vacations. When his year drew near to its end he found himself on the University examining board, setting and correcting papers and having a say in the final results of graduating students, a responsibility which he carried out adequately and sensibly. The University wrote and asked if they could retain him for a second year. This was not possible, but the students made their gratitude to him plain.

I had a very pleasing experience at the end of last term. Two classes both presented me with a very nice present and a representative of each gave a speech thanking me for my devotion and conscientious work with them during the term. One of the things that has impressed me here is the wonderful spirit among the students. They are hard-working, but they know how to relax and enjoy themselves together as a community. I couldn't hope for better friends and more enjoyable company.

In one basic particular the experience of the volunteer I shall call Dick was the same as John's, he too was alone on his project; in every other way it was very different.

When Dick first heard that he was to go on a particularily exciting assignment, the only European member of staff in an all African school in Swaziland, he was appalled. For twenty-four hours everything hung in the balance while Dick and his family made up their minds whether or not to withdraw from the scheme, and finally a very subdued Dick telephoned to say that he had decided to go ahead. This was, for him, the nadir; after this he never looked back.

Swaziland was one of the three British Protectorates lying within Southern Africa in a vulnerable and vital position. Dick was going to the government secondary school, a school with a Zulu headmaster and situated 'just at the foot of the hills where the ancient kings are buried.' Out of this school would come a high percentage of all young Swazis with any higher education, and probably most of the future administrators and officials. The school was mixed, taking both boys and girls, a fact that was at first rather an embarrassment to Dick.

As you can go to school as early as six years old and as late as fourteen there tends to be a great difference in age in each form. The boys and girls, therefore, tend to be anything up to twenty-two years of age. The boys (or some of them) have moustaches and wispy little beards! . . .

I have the doubtful pleasure of supervising the hundred girls for three hours prep once a week! The first time was quite an experience. Within seconds I had nine of them round me asking about some small point in the 'Doctor's Dilemma' which we had been doing that morning. You can guess how the others reacted and the sort of sound they made!

Besides teaching a full programme he took over many of the outdoor activities.

When I arrived I found that physical training consisted of them just flapping their arms around, so I soon put a stop to this. Now they are doing some really tough training to get them fit, press-ups, etc. I find that they really enjoy this: before it was a drudgery.

The soccer season is just coming to an end here, but I have played a few games with them. Some of them have a lot of ability but no idea of position play. Some of the boys play in bare feet, some in gym shoes and some in football boots, but it is mostly one thing on one foot and another on the other! Some play in shorts and braces!

By now all the qualms about his position had quite vanished away. The kindness of the headmaster and the staff soon put him at his ease and he now even faintly resented having European visitors intruding on 'his' territory!

I feel that my opportunity to do something useful here lies in the wonderfully unique position I am in—the only European at the school. In London I hated the thought of it, but now I am just thrilled that it is so. This means that wherever I go it is always with an African. I am one more link in the chain that is joining the two colours together. I feel right in the heart of the problem that is challenging the whole of this continent.

70

There were, however, problems more immediate and tangible to deal with. African schools, perhaps affected by the tense, stirring political atmosphere which so often surrounded them, were sometimes the scene of more or less serious upheavals. Dick had been warned about this, and given an illustration in the first-hand experience of a volunteer in Ghana. Neither he nor we, however, had thought that he would so soon find himself in a similar position.

NIGERIAN
SCHOOLBOY

I have left to the end of this letter the thing that has really caused excitement here for the last week or so. The first Thursday I was here I was officially welcomed by the staff and was called upon to make a speech saying exactly how I came to be here. So I told them all about the scheme and, by way of a joke, mentioned that a Ghana school had gone on strike and rioted and had to be closed down. Naturally I said that I hoped this would not happen to me!

Well, soon enough, it happened, and I nearly had the same experience! On Monday October 3rd, it was a public holiday here so there was no school. One of the boys got drunk and insulted one of the members of the staff. He was expelled on the Wednesday and that evening the students, instead of doing their prep, held a mass meeting and decided to strike. So next morning, Thursday, they demanded that the principal and the staff should meet the whole school in the Assembly Hall for a kind of 'slanging match'! Naturally this was not acceptable to us, so the principal told them that they should send a delegation to him with their complaints. This they refused to do, and thus came about a sit-down strike—for they all refused to go to their classrooms to be taught and just sat down on the grass! There was not much that could be done about this as there does not seem to be any sort of discipline here, nor any sort of effective punishment to enforce discipline. In fact expulsion is the only thing as corporal punishment is very rarely used.

In the middle of the morning the strikers marched over to the teacher training school to get them out on strike too. They refused as their exams are very soon and they could not afford it. The principal decided that the situation was beyond his control, so he called in the District Commissioner, who is chairman to the Board of Governors. The District Commissioner called the school together and told them that they must either send a delegation to the Board of Governors, or put their complaint in writing. By this time all the Governors had arrived and the strikers must have derived immense satisfaction from the number of smart cars! The District Commissioner made a very poor speech, as he is very inexperienced, and was 'hissed' from the hall.

Thus it was left for the students to decide whether to put down the complaints in writing or send a delegation. They then kept the Governors waiting for two hours before they eventually decided to send a delegation which was to consist of twenty of them! However, the Board of Governors then decided to meet them on the next Tuesday, as it was too late in the evening. Until then the students were to go back to work. This they did, but spent most of the time planning out what they were going to say to the Governors.

So the Governors met on Tuesday at 9.00 a.m. They did not come out from the meeting until 5.30 p.m., after no lunch and only ten minutes for tea! The delegation was with them for a mere three hours. Apparently all the students did was to throw mud at all the staff in turn—all lies! Their view of the expulsion was that two people of equal standing, teacher and boy, had had a quarrel and the boy had been expelled to please the teacher! The staff have no power really here—less power than a prefect in England!

The matter was settled by the students apologising and having to go to school on the Saturday, which is normally free. This was all. So nobody was really punished, the ring leaders were not found, and the staff had been attacked behind their backs. However the Board were satisfied.

We then had two pretty lengthy staff meetings to discuss all this. I was convinced that there was only one thing to do and that was to start getting some discipline into the place. We had to show that the staff were the bosses and to be obeyed. Everyone agreed, so we are now having a campaign to get on top of the students who before did much as they pleased. There are no responsible prefects, so we have to be prefects and staff. One thing which was notable during the strike was that there was no violence at all, unlike most of the strikes in the Union. If there had been it is almost certain that the school would have been closed down.

Now that they have settled down I find I have a lot of work to do — and correcting forty exercises every time takes a lot of effort.

Later:

I pride myself that I have completely reorganised the system of prefects here. Before there was chaos — we did not have a strong body of prefects and we had 'house captains', elected by the students themselves, being responsible for the discipline of the school. Anyway we had a couple of three-hour staff meetings and I plugged away solidly with my proposals and finally won. Now we have six school prefects and have restricted the power of the 'house captains' and 'form monitors'.

Six months ago I could not have conceived that I should be doing work as fascinating as this. I only hope that they are benefiting as much as I am.

Assistant District Officer

There was a wide variety of jobs which did not involve teaching as such; though an element of teaching — and learning — entered into all.

Patrick, whose aeroplane had to jettison fuel on his outward journey, went to Bechuanaland to act as an Assistant District Officer. One or two countries asked for volunteers for this work and, in some ways, it was the most 'orthodox' of the requests. In a sense, for the British, this was the continuation of their long association with countries overseas, and the automatic picture which sprang into the mind of anyone connected with the old colonial world when young men were mentioned was that of the cadet, going out to some remote out-station to carry on the work of administering the land. In this sense it was also the job which perhaps came nearest, for the volunteer, to the romantic imagined image of his early determination to spend this year overseas.

This concept had its drawbacks. Though these young men might appear, outwardly, to conform closely to the old pattern of the cadet, in actual fact the ethos which they brought with them was very different, and while prepared to work loyally for their superiors they felt themselves to owe also other loyalties which might sometimes conflict. On the whole the volunteers were happiest when they found themselves working away from the government centres where there was often an attitude of mind that they found hard to agree with, and a paternal solicitude for their welfare which made them very impatient.

Bechuanaland, another of the southern African Protectorates, covered immense areas of dry, and often barren, land. Its people were cattle owners, and the economy of the country revolved around the cattle, but it also supplied labour for the mines in South Africa, a fact which created problems for the families left behind.

Patrick soon showed himself sensible and responsible which meant that a great many jobs of varying importance were immediately turned over to him. Of these the collecting of taxes was a constant worry – the native of Bechuanaland being no more inclined to enjoy paying taxes than anyone else.

My work continues to be interesting and something new crops up every day. Since I last wrote I have been out on several tours, helping with a revision of the tax registers. This is often a dullish job, but it can have its amusing moments. The co-operation of the village headman is rather essential but in this particular area village headmen are notorious cattle thieves! The issue is further complicated by tax allowances for men with two or more wives! This job involved sitting for long, hot hours in the 'kgotla', calling out unpronounceable names and attempting to ascertain the whereabouts of defaulters. There seemed to be three stock answers: 'He's at the lands,' 'He's gone to the mines,' or more often than not, 'We don't know.' I was quite glad to get into the bush again towards the end of September.

Having been granted the use of a new government truck, I was able to become completely independent at last. I spent a week paying off pensioners in an area north of Francistown along the Rhodesian border. I started the journey with £1,400 in cash in the cubby-hole and two unguarded prisoners in the back, both awaiting trial for murder. It was quite a relief when the latter were safely locked in the Francistown gaol and the cash all paid out – even more so when I subsequently learned that about £1,000 was missing from the Treasury at Serowe! (This turned up a few days later.)

In October I began what has been my most interesting job so far – namely organising famine relief measures in one of the worst hit areas north of Francistown. After a year of drought and the recent outbreaks of foot and mouth disease, the people have become desperate for food, and as a result famine relief measures were brought in in certain areas. My main concern was getting bags of mealie meal to fourteen schools in out-lying villages, and arranging feeding schemes for each one.

In November I also spent a week or so holding meetings at the villages, trying to explain to the people what will happen when the Protectorate changes to a decimal currency next February. For the most part they said they would wait until the change took place before even trying to learn the details! This was all very well, but it didn't say much for my teaching! At one of these meetings I was somewhat taken aback to find a crowd of about four hundred sullen-looking men awaiting my arrival. It turned out that they had not come with the slightest idea of learning about decimalisation, but instead they subjected me to a barrage of complaints about the starvation. 'First you kill our cattle (foot and mouth) and now you're trying to kill us!' 'Our country's collapsing,' 'We cannot plough, our cattle are dying,' etc., etc. It became quite an embarrassing situation and increasingly difficult to think of suitably compromising answers!

Not too far away, in Barotseland which is a part of Northern Rhodesia, Roger was also coping with the finances of local government, and not finding it an easy job. Where Patrick was able to accept the policies of the Bechuanaland Government and enjoyed his work, Roger lived in a state of frustration, often shocked by what he saw done. He was a boy of great intelligence who rebelled strongly against the traditional pattern which he found in Central Africa. Where Patrick succeeded in breaking out of this and forging, although with some difficulty, a middle path in the delicate situation of race relations, Roger was dogged in all his endeavours to talk in an ordinary manner with Africans by the fact that he worked for the government and so was automatically a 'bwana', a master.

At the end of my first fortnight I was put on to helping compile the Barotse Native Government estimates. This should really be a District Commissioner's job and proved complex and hard, but most satisfying. The difficulty lies in relating paper to reality. If, for example, an old village policeman, employed by the Barotse Native Government, dies in a Native Court seventy miles away across the marsh and is replaced by a young one, the Boma just does not learn the fact except by hearsay, or interrogation of distant relatives. At the end of the week I was so dissatisfied with the general vagueness of my information that I drove out to Leabui to interview the Chief Treasury clerk. The state of his books was a real eye-opener. He had only the vaguest of notions about the meaning of them and the implication of his figures. It was here, actually, that I gave an increment to two underpaid employees on the spot simply by altering the figures opposite to their names.

That was a concrete job to be done, and for that reason a satisfactory one; but the complexities of his situation were illustrated in another duty.

I have inspected the prison with the District Commissioner. It's a soulless, sandy square with four white, concrete buildings inside a high, barbed-wire fence, a weary guard at the gate and slow, white-clad figures moving around inside. We walked through the big gates and slowly across to the prisoners, lined up in four blocks, and standing silently at ease in their shapeless, black-arrowed uniforms. We walked down the line together, the Warden, the District Commissioner and I—three white men in clean, pressed shorts and smart, khaki bush shirts, all three of us taller than anyone else in the compound; and a vivid otherness, a sense of irrefutable and infinite superiority established itself between the prisoners and me. The fit lasted only perhaps a minute, and left me feeling bitterly ashamed of myself. I mention this only to illustrate the easy temptation towards conceit out here, which very few resist completely.

Tradition has it, however, that under the last management the prisoners were allowed home at weekends. If they were late in reappearing they were locked out as a punishment!

Compared to the situation in Central Africa where emotional and psychological factors complicated what was in any case an arduous job, Chris, in the Solomon Islands, had a straightforward task. The actual frustrations of the work were as numerous and as tiresome as in any developing country, but at least they were not complicated by racial tensions.

As in most 'simple' societies there was an age-old system of communal labour which had enabled villages or clans to group themselves together to undertake essential community work. This system continued to be used now to help villages acquire amenities which it would otherwise be impossible for the government to undertake, either because there was not enough money to provide such things for every village without some self-help, or because what the village wanted was on too small a scale or in too remote a part of the country to merit wholesale government subsidy.

For the last two months I've been working on a road for the Local Council. Unfortunately all their bridges had been washed away and I had to organise, or at least set up an organisation to replace seven large and several small bridges, and three or four fords.

The first six weeks the Council had no money, and all the work had to be done by the community on their one day a week; so I rarely slept in the same village on successive nights.

These six weeks could only be preparatory because not much progressive work can be done working from Tuesday to Tuesday, and we used to gather timber, or coral, or mark out and preliminarily brush the extension of the road. Then the Council held its annual meeting and voted enough money to pay regular labour and alloted to me a small launch so that I could go further than my walking and canoeing before.

However the villagers refused to labour for love or money, since they had previously worked for the Council and had not been paid. This was amply justified since they'd been told how to build a bridge, understood, but did it another way, their own 'easier' way. The first rainstorm swept their flimsy posts away and they were told to stop work immediately. There was a little more to it than that, for the Council has bungled the whole thing and paid some part of their wages and some nothing.

As there was so little money available anyway I felt we couldn't afford to put right all their grievances with money; besides nobody had a clear idea of their own grouse. The Council Headman concocted the plan to make them do their four days a month consecutively, and if this was ordered to all the villages concerned we could get all our labour free. We told them that if they provided us with a gang of labourers as originally requested, we wouldn't enforce this consecutive business — although the other islands do it as a matter of course. They saw the point and offered two gangs to work for one week each.

Now I've set the bridge-making in motion my little part is finished and I'm being succeeded by an able local man who's very adept at throwing bridges across rivers.

Youth Work

At first it had seemed that youth work, helping with clubs of all kinds and organising leisure activities for young people, could be the ideal project. What could be better for an energetic youngster with a wide variety of interests of his own than helping other youngsters to develop and enjoy their own interests? To other people, overseas, this also seemed a sensible pattern and requests began to come in from governments for volunteers to help with youth work.

ASIAN STUDENT

We were soon to discover that such projects were fraught with difficulties and required a boy with great self-confidence, and with the stability of temperament to withstand constant frustration. The whole setting of a volunteer doing youth work was much vaguer than that of one who had a definite position within an institution, or who went to a department with a pattern of work which covered the whole day. Often the actual work with youngsters did not start until the evening, or late in the afternoon, and this left the volunteer with an empty day to fill.

It could also happen that the volunteer found that he had to create his own job; to start clubs, to form groups, to inject ideas and vitality. He could do this — but it was not an easy task for a lad who was a stranger to the country in which he was to work, and often local specialist staff were so few and so overworked

78

that they had little time to give much guidance or help to a new youngster.

As time went on it became apparent that one of the ways to overcome this difficulty was for the volunteer to go out to a school, which gave him a fixed day-time job, but to spend his evenings and spare time with youth clubs. This was the solution adopted by North Borneo, and it meant that when the club had its failures and difficulties—as it inevitably did—the volunteer was not thrust into the depths of depression, because he still had his job in the school and because the work in the youth club was only one facet of his relationship with the local youngsters.

In some countries, however, youth clubs fulfilled a much more fundamental role. They did not just cater for leisure or hobbies but were full-time institutions, often deeply occupied with the problems of youngsters who were unemployed or not at school. In an under-developed country, where schooling was not necessarily compulsory but where rapid change-over in the economy made the land less and less a satisfactory occupation for many boys, the semi-educated youngster was an increasing problem; and there were often no mid-way training institutions or apprenticeship schemes to help absorb him into worthwhile work. In this situation the youth club could also make it its business to teach trades like motor mechanics or shoe repairing, as well as encouraging Scouts or games, giving the youngsters a centre which, in a small way, may have replaced the initiation schools for young men which many African tribes had in times gone by.

Kenya was a country which took this aspect of its youth work very seriously, but, as always, even in Britain, there was very little money for this particular department of Social Welfare. This meant that when the volunteers arrived they found themselves faced with very heavy responsibilities, to cope with which required a good deal of ingenuity and energy. This description of the work which Tony found himself engaged in gives some idea of its scope.

After a short while in Nairobi, the capital, where he learnt something about the way that the Kenya Government worked in these things and made the acquaintance of his boss, himself a young man of great energy and enthusiasm, Tony was moved up into a country district where he was to be responsible for starting a number of clubs. The plans had already been made and much of the work done, but shortage of staff to supervise had meant many delays.

At the moment we haven't started work properly, and we are being inaugurated into youth club work. However things are beginning to happen and this month I'm moving up to the Kambara District. When I reach my new home I shall take charge of a brand new club with a mixed capacity of about four hundred. My job will be to get the organisation of the club like clockwork and to introduce as many new ideas as possible. If I make a good job of this club, of which a great deal is expected, I shall take over about seven or eight more clubs by Christmas.

Later:

I begin this Thursday when I am meeting the boys already enrolled in the club with whom I am going to start a Scout troop, which will form the nucleus. These boys are being selected by the village elders and headmen, three from each village, giving a grand total of thirty-six. I am also having to swot up my Guiding, as I intend having a Girl Guide company, under the leadership of the lady club leader, who unfortunately knows nothing about Guiding.

Later:

The club is certainly open now, having at present a membership of two hundred and seventy-five, going up to three hundred and fifty in about another month or so. A film is being made of the club and myself by the Kenya Information Department. It covers all the various aspects of activities — except classroom work — ranging from morning inspection to Kikuyu dancing by the girls. They went into all the workshops taking pictures of bicycle repairing, shoe making and home craft, leaving out tailoring and carpentry as they felt these were rather 'everyday' things. Perhaps they are — to them and to you and I — but for these kids, my kids, they are things so far removed from the normal that they are prepared to walk perhaps five, six or even nine miles to do them, every day, come rain or shine.

Tony had the loan of a government jeep and he covered a lot of ground opening and supervising a number of clubs, all on similiar lines and catering for large numbers. That was in the country; in Nairobi another volunteer, Chris, was doing exactly the same thing but in an urban setting.

To begin with there were only two clubs in Nairobi, but soon after I arrived a school which was being run illegally was closed down by the Education Department. This meant that one hundred and fifty boys were running around Nairobi during the day. To solve this problem it was decided that I was to open a Youth Centre. My immediate problem was to open it and worry about the money later.

The day-to-day problems in this work were manifold, and they came both from above and from below. On the one hand there were the boys, volatile, unstable, sometimes delinquent, often from poverty-stricken homes: on the other insufficient finance, harrassed officials to be dealt with, and intermittent support. Perhaps only a very young man could have coped with all this and managed to retain gaiety and enthusiasm and some sense of purpose. Peter described his Christmas with his children out in a country area.

The day started early and while the children were eating the Christmas presents we gave them, my dog ate our breakfast. Chris and I devoured an enormous mince pie and set off to the mission with the boys, taking Chris's small motor-scooter with us. The service began at eight o'clock and went on for three hours. The local inhabitants brought up their collections including livestock. Of course my dog and a chicken met by the collection table in front, chaos for a few seconds, then the sudden retreat of the dog. The service was brought to an untimely end when a local agitator stood up to denounce all Europeans in Kenya. There was a hurried blessing and then we all filed out.

Chris and I then went off with the missionaries to the local prison and returned for a well-deserved lunch. The coffee was interrupted by a breathless report that 'pikipiki broken, sah!' Some of our little charges had found and then experimented with the motor-scooter. We told the guilty parties to wheel the machine back to camp, but we later discovered that the boys had got the engine going. I say this because I had to bail a boy out later at the local police station.

Eventually we led our little band home, all intact. We felt it had been a 'different' Christmas Day. The next morning we over-slept.

Jamaica was another country with a major youth unemployment problem. Behind its beautiful facade of a holiday island, Jamaica seethed with the difficulties of poverty and under development which brought so many of her people to Britain to seek for better jobs. One of the efforts to deal with unemployment among the young was the Jamaica Youth Corps, which took into its camps large numbers of jobless youngsters and gave them training in agriculture and trades as well as discipline, and an extra breathing space before they were cast on the country's economy. The first request from Jamaica visualised the volunteers being attached to the Youth Corps Camps as assistant staff, and they did, in fact, go out to this job. The situation, however, was a very flexible one and, once on the job, the volunteer was able to tailor his own project to suit his particular talents and inclinations—a proposition at once attractive and dangerous because it allowed such a wide latitude of choice.

Charlie went out for fifteen months. He was a boy of great charm, full of ideas and well able to convince those with whom he worked that they were good ones. He had also a valuable extra skill, he was a conjurer; and this talent sent the small Jamaican boys into such paroxysms of pleasure and laughter that Charlie occasionally feared that he might be responsible for their ending up, literally, in fits. They believed him to be possessed of magic powers and once, at least, he was asked to replace some lost teeth and had considerable difficulty in making a satisfactory explanation of his impotence which did not result in too much undermining of his position! His one disadvantage—according to Charlie himself—was that he came from a very famous school, which resulted in a surfeit of hospitable invitations; however, this too he managed to overcome without ill-feeling.

In Charlie and Jamaica there happened a rare combination from which resulted a genuine creative flowering, developed from the exact conjunction at the right moment of a volunteer with the one situation that supremely suited his gifts and temperament. The following extracts from his letters cover the whole of his stay in Jamaica and give some idea both of the development of the project and of its difficulties.

I feel that life is only just beginning for me out here. Each day I learn something more and meet new experiences, and each day I feel that I am meeting with more response in handling these boys. . .

The camp here is young and is very badly staffed. At first I kept pretty mum, just watching and learning. By the end of June

I had gained the campers' confidence entirely and they trusted me and told me everything. I was in a tricky position, trying not to let the staff down and yet trying to be just. Sometimes the campers were at fault; sometimes the staff was. During May I had been as nice as I possibly could to the staff and they had been, in turn, very nice back; in the evenings we would chat and play dominoes. The boys were accepting me more and more, and I found myself every evening playing games with them or sitting in their dormitories having lengthy discussions or just joking and having fun. During the day I would chat gently to the boys as I went round seeing them all on the farm, showing them what to do and how to do it — I'm fairly good at Jamaican farming now! — praising them or criticising them when due — chiefly praising, as no one else in the camp ever did it.

I tried to help them and give them advice, explain to them why they had to do certain things, why a member of staff was cross with them, (they would say to me: 'Mr So-and-so has made me look small, sir.') why they must learn to be punctual, why they must learn to work conscientiously and so on. They no longer regarded me as really a full-time member of staff, just a friend.

Those far-off days were happy and peaceful, but a bit tame I now think. There was never a dull moment though as I gave myself no time to think at all. Then I struck! I hollered, and am still hollering. I think a little has happened, although you can't tell when you're in the midst of things yourself. The only conscious results to me are that I'm on much better terms with most of the staff as I've managed to fire them with a little enthusiasm.

Discipline didn't really exist, neither did punctuality. One morning breakfast had been ready for thirty minutes and no boy, no member of the staff. I locked the door and kept them waiting for an hour. They all thought me mad, but they weren't late again, staff as well! Campers had been getting off to work late and coming back early. The Director backed me up and vast fatigue gangs were organised. That worked too. And so it went on. Strange to say my relationship didn't really break with the boys. Some of them who suffered mumbled that I would make a hard policeman, and those who didn't suffer thoroughly enjoyed it all ... I think they admired me rather than hated me because they realised it was just. I was expecting a hard time! I suggested one or two alterations in the administration of the camp and they adopted one or two, but by this time it was very near to the end of the 'term' when the campers were leaving and I sat down to watching again and didn't holler quite so hard — except to keep the discipline.

Campers come here from all over Jamaica and often wear shoes for the first time, and use a spoon and fork for the first time to eat. By the time they leave, after a year, we hope they are very different. They ought to be even more different than they are, but often they cannot go home to the country — their standard of living has changed so much. They leave, and all security goes. They must find work in the seas of unemployment here and it is so easy to sink and lose what they have learnt, and they are very conscious of what they have learnt, most of them taking education of any kind very seriously.

So, during July, they had begun to get worried about this approaching uncertainty. The Corps cannot possibly find employment for one thousand boys annually, but gives each camper a genuine recommendation and fills any vacancies they are asked to fill with their best campers. So most of July was taken up with warning the leavers and trying to console them and advise them. Not many got very moody, but some did and you just had to get them to do something to take their minds off it for a while after a little chat . . .

Towards the end of July one hundred and twenty campers left for good and half the rest went on leave — leaving about seventy-five. I was very sorry to part with so many good friends. Pace in the camp slowed down and I could almost relax for a few days . . .

Later:

I have at last managed to get a sort of car, and I filled it up with boys and rolled down to the annual National Agricultural Show in the centre of the island. Then I spent a fortnight at a camp just outside Montego Bay, bathing in the lucious warm, pebbly sea. The first week was little boys who were great fun and the second week a bunch of forty delinquents, from fifteen to twenty years old. And they were fascinated by my colour. I think I must be the first Englishman of their own age, who was prepared to know them and become friends, that they had met, and they pummelled me with questions. I had had a little of it at the camp and knew the ropes, but I had never had an onslaught like this. 'Why do the whites hate us?' 'When will the black/white war be?' Fantastic

questions, unceasing all the while I was there. I had to push them
off to meals. They knew very little and were only half educated,
and I tried to tell them as much as I could. How much they understood or believed I don't know. They seemed interested. For
instance they don't know the difference between English, Americans, French or Russians and think us all the same. They believe
that they look like Africans — they have all as much white blood
as black in them. One boy was fairer than I and called himself
coloured, which began to make them think what was the difference.
They had a great inferiority and hatred complex, quite blind,
against the English and were much more colour conscious than
any Englishman I've met . . .

Later:

I've just had a letter. I'm to be Area Officer for the Youth
Club Council on the North Coast among my delinquents. I'll
probably go within a month. It will be extremely exciting — I only
hope I can do the job. I expected to help someone, but one man's
got the sack (I think) and so I've got to look after all the clubs
in one of the six areas. It will be wonderful to be my own master;
but I shall be very sorry to leave these boys . . .

Later:

Here now, in Falmouth, I've got quite a job to do but it's a job
which you cannot rush and in which you spend hours getting from
place to place. In two or three months I've got to try to 'build'
about twenty clubs, and as these clubs at the moment meet only
once a week it makes it all the slower. But the hardest task of all
is to find leaders, first of all who are genuinely interested in youth
work and haven't got too much on their plate already, and secondly
someone who will do it for nothing — the same old story. In most
places the school teacher is the leader if he is not already too
busy — in the country parts they have to do everything including
burying the dead.

There are plenty of people of the upper-middle and upper
classes willing to sit on councils, etc., and some are extremely
generous financially but practically no one who is suitable will
actually lead a club. This week I've spent nearly all my time in
Falmouth itself. This is a town of about four thousand people and
is dead. It was at one time, the turn of the nineteenth century, an

extremely prosperous new town thriving on the trade of sugar — formerly it had existed as a small pirate hide. Now a ship comes into the tiny harbour less than once a month. The whole town is surrounded by a swamp which is slowly, very slowly, being reclaimed. Unemployment is vast. Some have found jobs in Montego Bay twenty-two miles away, the rest just buy and sell to each other, or do nothing. The town is dead, as quiet as a mouse, which for Jamaica is unique. Normally they love noise and really know how to give a party — but not in Falmouth.

'Dere just nutting to do, sa,' one boy said to me. I've fired the boys' imaginations and I think that while I'm here all will go well. I've talked about swimming clubs and hiking clubs and cricket and football clubs, singing and debating societies and so on, and at the moment they seem very interested. Most of them are bored delinquents and I was surprised at their response, although from the moment I came into town late on Sunday night I realised life was going to be much easier than I expected. One boy happened to see me and shouted to me and I stopped and talked with him. Soon my car was completely surrounded and I could only move on with promises I would see them all next day. But I wasn't going to have it so easy. Later another ten barged into my little room wringing my hand again and again thankful to see me from the camp. I think they rather regard me as a sort of guardian angel now. At camp they liked me I think — most of them — but I was very much a white man and far away from them. Some especially, who very much distrusted me because of my skin and the way some white people act out here, now could not be nicer. They think I am going to restore the town to its former glory just like that. They are all worried about the place and in despair that I will only be here about three months.

'You can do good to de town, sa, but you can't do good to de town in dat time.'

No man can help this town to prosper until the swamps are drained. All I can do is comfort the dying in organising a little pleasure which might continue when I go, although the boys say they will 'strike' then! Life is going to be painfully slow but it is fascinating meeting all the people I am meeting and will meet . . .

In the morning I do a little office work and there's always something else to do in Falmouth as unemployment is high and some of the boys are tough, although they melt a bit to me because of my

colour with my slap-happy cheerfulness — its a little false but it's
what they like. If you slap a boy hard over the back and make a
joke you've got him where you want him. Their lives are empty
and I don't know why they don't do more crime than they do. To
say a few words to any boy may make his day . . .

Later:

These last three months have gone spinning by all too quickly.
By the New Year I was settled into Falmouth and could start
doing something. All the boys are very mixed up, with odd com-
plexes, feeling unwanted in this world as they are cursed off for
their deplorable behaviour by 'everyone of standing' and mostly
are unemployed. Still we have now in Falmouth the only 'Youth
Centre' in the island which is purely for the youth of Falmouth.
It's an old warehouse, built in the days of slaving, which we got
for an indefinite period from the owner as no one was using it.
It is now open four times a week and I hope soon five times. The
boys wired it and carried out mountains of luggage, cut bamboo
and made a fence round a concreted outside, made seats and a
canteen bar, whitewashed everything in sight including themselves,
and even dug up the road outside to put a drain across. We had a
very nice opening and I managed to get eight leaders to take it in
turns to be there when it is open, and I hope and pray that it will
work. At the moment the question is funds to buy more gear and
wood to make the tables and stools, and I am trying to get the
kids themselves to raise the money instead of begging it, so that
they have some pride in it.

At the end of February I had a leaders training course which I
think went down well and the leaders certainly learnt something.
It was the first one to be held here. At the end of March I had an
Athletic Meet in Falmouth for all the club members which everyone thoroughly enjoyed, but it was killing to get the thing to come
to pass. With great difficulty I got my boys, or some of them to
do a little for themselves and cut their own track, but even then
many watched me do it! . . .

The work is the greatest fun and I don't think I could possibly
want any other job in any other country in the world. It is tiring
often, not getting in until ten o'clock at night, and there are long
distances over rough roads, but the work is satisfactory. It's an uphill struggle all the way but I feel I am doing something, although it

is very little — I feel I am creating something which, I hope, will continue when I'm gone.

Community Development

Projects with Community Development had all the glamour — at least when viewed from Britain — of dealing with remote peoples in jungle surroundings. They combined the attraction of being a jack-of-all-trades with a sense of urgency, of harnessing the twentieth century on behalf of simple peoples suddenly confronted by it. In effect, and on the spot, community development could take many forms and could, at times, be quite as arduous, routine and exasperating as any other project. In most cases it was essential, because of the nature of the work, that some attempt be made to learn the local language — and this the volunteers set out to do in the same way that they learned to mix cement and bud rubber, for the greater efficiency of the job.

Colin arrived one evening, very late, at our home. My husband was out and while I gave Colin a cup of tea I tried to discover what had brought him so suddenly upon us.

It was near the end of holidays and he was returning to school in a few days time. It was not hard to find out why he was there: he was quite ready to tell me. He had heard of the experiences of a boy from his own school, at that moment serving in Sarawak, and he had come to say that he, Colin, wished to volunteer and to go to the most remote and primitive of all the places we could find. I teased him gently about his conviction that he could undertake a job in a place as wild and far-flung as he was imagining, but he did not respond. He simply sat there, waiting for my husband, determined that he was going to get overseas, and saying, 'If Richard can do it, I can do it too.'

My husband did not come in until after eleven o'clock, and Colin was still there, prepared if necessary to ignore me and wait all night.

Some weeks later there came a request from the Government of British Guiana for a volunteer, which we were forced to read twice, so startling was what it proposed. In effect it asked for a youngster who would go and live in one of the Amerindian Reserves to help build up, from the very beginning, a community development programme. British Guiana, a small country on the north-east seaboard of South America, had a mixed population. On the coast many originally immigrant peoples, of Negro, Indian, mixed Spanish and other races, were moving rapidly, if rather erratically, towards self-government. But in the interior, as so often, the indigenous peoples, the Amerindians, driven further and further into the wild land, were gradually being overwhelmed. They had remained until very recent times, as indeed had the Dayaks in Sarawak, unaffected by the civilisation which was creeping up the coasts. But now, suddenly, it seemed that this could no longer be so and the consciences of the British administrators were, too late, roused by the recognition that these people were totally unable to meet the fate which was rushing towards them and might very well be annihilated by it. So a crash programme was to go into action to try to give the Amerindian some idea how a money economy worked, of local government, of education, in the hope that, somehow, he might be enabled to hold his own when self-government arrived.

But there were few staff to do this, and it was not a job that could be done half-time or a few days a week.

It was proposed that the volunteer should go up and live on the reserve, building his own house, and spending his entire time introducing the Amerindians to various self-help schemes. He would be quite alone, with the nearest European fifty miles away, but they would give him a speed-boat so that he could keep in touch.

We wrote and asked if they realised that our volunteers were eighteen and came straight from school.

They replied that they did; and added that a generation before young men not so very much older would also have gone out to administer large tracts of land without any previous experience, and had often done so with conspicuous sense, fairness and devotion.

We answered that we would send them a volunteer.

When the moment came to make the vital decision as to who should undertake this difficult and responsible project we gave it much thought. It was, in any case, policy that volunteers worked as individuals and not in a group, at most that two worked together, but this needed a young man who could spend much of his time quite alone, and who possessed sufficient internal resources to maintain in these circumstances not only his balance but also his creative energy. Inevitably our discussions came to Colin; his conviction that he could survive in a job which was remote, his determination to let no obstacle stand in his way of achieving this, and his intelligence and friendliness. After long deliberation we posted him to Orealla, and he more than vindicated this decision.

He arrived in September, and for the first three months he went about learning as much as he could, as fast as he could, about British Guiana, the Amerindians, and community development.

This last month has been a wonderful experience. Almost the whole of the area is swamp savannah, and the Amerindians live scattered up and down the river on small islands. So all the travel is by boat—it is wonderful to see children paddling their way down to school, at the age of five or six, completely self-possessed! I'm becoming quite expert at paddling their corials (canoes).

I have been moving around with the local Assistant District Commissioner, attending local council meetings, etc., to see a bit of their way of life under his guidance. But I'm really working on my own now: there's never a spare moment as there's so much to do, and what I'm trying to do is very slow work. I'm afraid I was not born patient—but already I'm amazed at the patience which has been hammered into me by force of circumstances. The Amerindians are very responsive while one is on the spot: but completely unreliable when you're not. They'll agree with you entirely: and then do nothing about it! This poses a bit of a dilemma in a way as it means one has to be permanently leading them: whereas I feel that the real purpose of anything I do is to teach them to lead themselves. This is the very thing they are unable to do at the moment: and I think it has been mainly because of government policy towards them. Living in reserves which no outsiders are allowed to enter, they are having no experience of the outside world, and while this lasts they can never learn how to deal with it. And while government organises everything for them, they can never learn to look after themselves: and it is this which makes them unreliable and lazy.

Lazy they may be, but that doesn't detract from their charm! And I am really very lucky in my status as a non-official: it means that I really do things among them, instead of from above. In practice, e.g. this means that if I organise some meeting I don't go to it by motor-boat, but I paddle there with one of them in a corial. If they get soaked by a storm, then I do too. They sense this very quickly: and so now that I am getting to know them all personally, they tell me whatever they think.

February:

Now for Orealla — I've been here nearly a month now; I was certainly glad to get here, as the place was beginning to have an increasingly mythical quality for me! One of the Assistant District Commissioners spent the first week with me and was very good value — both by way of introducing me to the people and the local issues — and especially for his yarns in the evening. Meanwhile my house is just about finished, and the boathouse, with a sixty foot ramp to lower the boat — it's a wonderful little launch, and fairly easy to handle now that I'm used to it, eighteen foot long, with seventy horse power behind it — so it only takes me about an hour and a quarter to cover the fifty miles to the river mouth. The house is going to have a magnificent view: it would have been finished by now, but for the fact that the saw-miller from whom I ordered the boards tried to pull a fast one on me — the Amerindians who are building the house were wild!

'Look Chief, is pure scrap the sampy coolie-man (East Indian) bring — we going to mash him with cutlass an' throw him in the river' — and they nearly did!

There is a lot of routine work here, as I'm the only person stationed here and they come running to you if there's a hope of sympathy — everything from complaints about the wife to logging disputes and keeping the rum off the reserve, as the Amerindians are forbidden it. Other than this we've got a little committee going, which meets once a fortnight and should become a proper village council in a few months; they are working right now on a cattle pasturage in the bush, and we have plans for drainage, as erosion is a very real problem here.

April:

I can hardly keep my eyes open, after what began as an evening meeting and ended almost as an all-night session with our local housing society — which I don't believe I've told you about before, as it's a scheme we've only just started in the last few weeks. Several of the men here wanted to build new houses this year so I got them together, just to see if they could do the work together at first, and then when their interest seemed to be going up in leaps and bounds I thought it worth a self-help scheme which has just been passed. These 'self-help schemes' are the main factor in development projects out here, whereby government provides all the materials for a scheme and the people themselves provide the labour, which has to be at least up to the level of government assistance. Anyway, our housing scheme for nine families has just been approved with a grant of 2,000 dollars – but almost the whole of the cost will be on boards, so there's none for technical assistance, and I am desperately trying to remember a few of my school carpentry lessons! We're starting on it next week, with the men working in two groups, of five and four.

Of course, whenever anyone has a job to be done here, he has what is called a masromani – he gives the drink and you give the work, the drink being bamboli, their local brew from a root, which is chewed and spat into a jug by the old women! And that is how these men will probably work – and they promised to finish it before the 'chief' goes back to England. But these schemes are the devil to run in a closed community like this, though fascinating at the same time – one of them thinks that so-and-so doesn't want to work, so he's not going to, or A simply doesn't get on with B so he won't work if B is working – or someone comes and tells them that they've done something badly or wrong, and in a flash they're gone – but once they get interested in a thing they're just like children, and they can't stop . . .

Great triumph, as we've just finished one scheme – building a 'stelling', as they call it out here – a pier – which was another self-help scheme, and took us about a month with about twenty men working each day: and pretty heavy work too, as it involved hulking enormous wooden frameworks about with no equipment at all, and having to work with the tide, as it comes right up the river here from the sea. However, it's really finished now, and they're so proud of it that they just want to sit there all day!

It's terrific fun working with them, and they're so proud of what they do and have a wonderful sense of humour, bantering with each other the whole day long – and every day a huntsman had to go out to shoot something for breakfast (lunch!) and was solemnly thrown off the end if he came back empty handed!

Life here seems to get better than ever – the local committee are doing splendidly, and have really mastered the technique of holding meetings, and much more important, of putting their decisions into effect. Also we've just completed the census which is being taken for the whole Caribbean, and I had to supervise it for the whole river, which was a terrible bore but really made worthwhile by one incident alone – by Alberga Kelly (from Nicaragua!) a real wild bushman living alone in the far reaches of the river, who, when I came to the third census question, which was whether he was married, replied that he had shot four men and if any damned white man came and asked him dirty questions he'd make it five! The rest of his census paper, I need hardly add, reads as a blank!

I love this place – right on a sweeping bend on the river, completely timeless and peaceful, where no one can get at you to bother you about anything. And before you've been here any time you lose your heart to the Indians – especially the children – I've really made some of the greatest friends of my life among them – and just normal friends, as for instance one was friends with a person at school. I think it will be quite a break for me to leave here.

July:

What sort of qualities does he need – my successor? That is a big question, and I feel I would be a better person if I had found my way to the answer. I'll list a few that occur to me if you like – patience, the willpower never to give up, the ability to get on with any type of person, however different that person may be from his own background, to win trust among simple minds and always be aware of what these minds will be thinking, to learn from experience, to take on a lot of administrative responsibilities, and have no prejudices – and not least of all the ability to handle an axe, shoot straight, climb trees, and deal with outboard motor and radio-telephone equipment . . . if you can get someone who can do all this, the situation should be well in hand!

But seriously, though they are really rather abstract things to look for, I think the most important are – to be able to make friends with anyone, to take on quite a lot of responsibility, to improvise in almost any situation, and to learn by experience – and not least of all, which I almost forgot because I have come to take it for granted now, is that he will have to accept the fact of living alone, which I feel will be the first hurdle that anyone who takes on here will have to clear. And it makes me realise that I must have grown a little older in the last year to be able to take so much for granted that I got it last!

I can hardly grasp the fact that I'll really be turning homewards in a couple of months. I think it's the fact of never talking to anyone about England — except the Amerindians, of course — that makes it hard for me to believe that England still exists! Not that I've ever been homesick since I left, which shows that I must have enjoyed it. I really think it's going to break my heart to leave here — no more of the children, of the Indian banter, of their parties too, and the life on the river. It's very exciting to see a little of our efforts bearing fruit — our local council is now really standing on its own feet, and I can sit back at their meetings without saying a word, and everything runs smoothly — they are even taking their duties so seriously that one of them proposed the other day that the term 'uncle' should not be used in addressing other members of the council at a meeting! Needless to say, the proposal was rejected, but I had a good chuckle about it. The housing scheme is going well too and six of the nine men have nearly completed their houses — the hardest thing has been to keep them working together, as Albert will come to me one day and tell me,

'Chief, James got a way by heself, he no want to work with me at all,' or Eric will say that Albert 'been sie bad word open me and me no stody for work with he at all,' etc!

The latest news from here is that I may not get back at all — the Indians have been bewailing about the day when I go back for a long time now and I heard today that the local piai man — witch-doctor — has a plan to keep me back here. Apparently he has only to get a copy of my footprint, which won't be very difficult, as one hardly wears shoes out here, and I simply can't leave without the word from him.

September: A postcard written in New York on the way home.

Just to let you know that I really did persuade myself to leave — though not without many hours of song and dance and a few tears as an end to it all. It has been a wonderful year. I never knew that life could be so rewarding as it has proved in these last months.

Colin handed over to Julian, another eighteen-year-old, before he left, and Julian carried on the work that had been begun. After that the increasingly uncertain political situation of the country put difficulties in the way of a continuing supply of volunteers. Nevertheless, for Colin, this was a beginning and not an end, and he retained and developed his deep interest in the problem of the Amerindians and his great affection for them.

Apprentices

Originally both thinking and action in the plans for Voluntary Service Overseas had been confined to the school-leaver. But after the first year, with the recognition that the young had a special contribution to make to many of the social problems of the twentieth century world, we began to think not in particular categories of youngsters but on a much broader basis.

This led my husband to the revolutionary concept that the young apprentice, with a technical skill to offer, might well have a part to play. The idea that these young men, earning good money, already within the promotion framework of their profession and coming from a background quite divorced from any sense of traditional service in countries overseas, might be prepared to volunteer to spend a year helping without pay was considered ludicrous by many. That their firms would be prepared to let them go seemed equally far-fetched.

The arguments, however, for their inclusion in an endeavour of this kind seemed to us very powerful. All too often in situations overseas which demanded a degree of technical skill the link was missing between the highly-paid, highly-qualified engineer and' the humble local workman. Somewhere in the middle echelon jobs frequently became unstuck because there was no one with a sufficient degree of technical skill who was ready to work alongside those actually engaged in the project, helping, teaching and maintaining standards. In colonial days the Public Works Department had not been noted for enlightened views on the part of its expatriates. The concern, so often, of the white man who went overseas with a technical skill was to dissociate himself as much as possible from the local technician, rather than to establish links through their common crafts.

Through the apprentice, this was the chance to make 'technical aid' real to the man in the street: to make it possible for the ordinary young man in industry to feel that he, personally, could have a stake in this kind of assistance to the under-developed countries, either by going himself, or by being a member of an apprentice group which had 'our Stan in Sarawak' or 'our Jim in Jamaica'. And for the firm this was a chance to give their up-and-coming young men the opportunity to adapt themselves to fresh situations, to emerge from what could be a narrow world and find out how other people lived, and to return with experience and maturity ready to take responsibility. It would also, on a more practical level, do a firm no harm to have its apprentices seen working in countries overseas with which it might well have trade relationships.

In theory we were ourselves convinced of the value of this idea: it remained, however, to find out whether it would prove acceptable in practice.

The first firm approached, Associated Electrical Industries, agreed to the scheme more out of surprise than from conviction. The chairman had thought that my husband was making a plea for money, and when asked instead for two of his apprentices was stunned into agreement. Perhaps relief that this was not just another appeal to the firm's pocket also played some part in his acceptance in principle of the idea! It was made plain to us, however, that there must be consultation at all levels and that any disagreement would immediately rule out participation. Some weeks later my husband was again summoned to the Head Office and told that, to the surprise of the hierarchy, this proposal had received a bigger response from the educational and training personnel than any put forward since the war.

The next step was to choose the apprentices. A.E.I. conducted the first part of the selection with great thoroughness and care. When volunteers were asked for, a large number of the apprentice force had come forward; letters were then sent round to all their parents asking if they were agreeable to their son going before a board, and explaining very carefully that, if he were chosen, a

OUTDOOR CLASS

considerable sacrifice in pay would be asked of the young man. When my husband went up to make the final selection he was shown the replies to this letter. They were heart-warming. Every one expressed pride that their boy should wish to do this and might have the chance of going overseas; and every one was prepared to accept the financial sacrifice involved in his doing so.

Eventually David and Peter were chosen and both came down to London to spend a night with us before setting off to Kenya, which was their posting. It was a tremendous step for them. Dressed in new clothes, their tools and their overalls in their suitcases they were setting out for a world which might almost have been the moon for all their previous knowledge of it. Even London and our home was a strange and exciting experience, and one of them described, with endearing simplicity, how as the train drew out of Manchester, and his mother's face receded down the platform, he had felt suddenly, for the first time, what it was like to leave family and home and had found himself in tears.

David went to a Christian Industrial Training Centre in a slum district of Nairobi where an attempt was made to teach a trade to boys who left school at fourteen but could not get work until they were sixteen and so were otherwise ripe for an idle, and eventually delinquent, life. David was the technical instructor and he quickly found that his job included not only teaching but bargaining for his materials in the markets, making blueprints for jobs, seeking profitable work which the boys could do and so contribute towards the expenses of the centre, as well as a number of activities unconnected with his technical skills.

The school is divided into three classes of A.B.C.: the class C is boys who have a low educational standard and cannot speak very good English. So they do no practical work for the first year but stay in the classrooms doing English, maths and varying handicrafts. Class B. and A. are older boys and they do half a day practical and half a day theory. When they are doing their practical they use the new workshop which is open-air and of very modern design. The class is split in two, one half doing general engineering training and the other half carpentry. I work on the engineering side, apart from which I take a class or two for sport or boxing, which goes very well with all the boys. And on Saturday we run a boys' club with all English games.

He was not very articulate on paper, but he was competent and imaginative in action. He designed the blueprint for a boat that the boys could make, converted an old fire-engine, and, above all, made friends. His boys grew as fond of him as he of them and, at a time when most Europeans preferred not to walk about the slums or pay visits to poor African homes, David was welcome and accepted in both places.

Peter went into a different kind of project. Kenya laid great emphasis on youth work, both in a government and a Christian Council setting. One of the major problems of the country was a growing number of youngsters with a little schooling who could not find jobs, either because their qualifications were in fact not good enough, or simply because a new economy had not yet adjusted itself to an increasing drift from the land. In a country with a seriously disturbed political atmosphere these youngsters were an ever-present danger. Idleness could breed gangs, could be the background to delinquency, to rioting, to illicit trafficking of all kinds. It is also true to say that the average African youngster wanted to equip himself better for the wonderful twentieth-century world which he imagined was just around the corner, and so there was a real thirst for extra education of all kinds. All these factors made the work of the youth clubs of great importance, and, unlike Britain, they operated twenty-four hours a day, running classes in such things as shoe-repairing and motor mechanics as well as sports and bands.

Peter went to help in such a club, and he very soon found himself administering it as well as instructing in it.

Let me explain what an ordinary day is like. The youth club starts at 8.30 a.m., stops at 12.00 p.m., then 2 to 4; 4 to 5 is games and sports. I do all the correspondence between the sponsors and the clubs. I visit firms in Nairobi to ask for material for the workshops. Today I got five tons of timber from a large firm. I'm learning more about the powers of persuasion. I have a great friend who has lent me transport whilst I stay here, now I can get three time as much work done in a day. One of his many jobs is to be manager of an African daily newspaper. My boys in the youth club deliver the paper in the morning before coming to school. We get three cents for each newspaper. If I can make this a big thing it will supply the money for more boys to be resident in the club. It takes me half a day to get the next day's order in, but! it is worth it if it goes.

Both my bands were playing last Saturday. One at the African stadium and the other at a small village sports outside Nairobi. My Swahili is getting a little better but I'm afraid I can't ramble yet.

For the boy who had hardly ever been outside Manchester before he was not doing badly!

It proved to be more difficult to find projects for apprentices which fully used their skills than we had anticipated. But there were many opportunities of a more ordinary nature in which the fact that they were craftsmen made them extra valuable. This kind of a job could be more of a test for the apprentice than trade training; it demanded great flexibility, and sufficient imagination to be able to adjust his own high degree of technical skill to a more humble level. In such situations he would be responsible only to himself for the standard of his work, and often with a whole community dependent on him for skilled solutions to their difficulties—but solutions which took note of primitive conditions.

Bob went from the Bristol Aeroplane Company to be 'handy man' to a mission working in a part of Kenya which had suffered severely from famine. He found himself distributing dried milk to children with protein deficiency, covering a large area in a Land Rover with a medical dresser accompanying him to hold small clinics. But Bob was not an engineer for nothing. He set himself to solve some of the problems that he saw around him.

The picture I enclose shows a battery of sun heaters which I have fixed up outside the children's ward (of the hospital). The insulated tank contains about sixty gallons, which is raised to 120° F on a sunny day. It has become quite a thing that the patients from other wards turn up in the children's ward in the late afternoon for a hot bath. Beauty of it is that one doesn't need any fuel and one doesn't have to mess about with fires. The whole thing works automatically by convection.

Hospitals seemed to offer a variety of possibilities. In Sierre Leone, on the west coast of Africa, Trevor, from the Southern Electricity Board, was an instructor at the Technical Institute in

Freetown, the capital. But in the holidays he travelled around and gave what help he could.

I spent a very interesting eleven days at the hospital at Segbarema. My jobs included such things as mending toys, false legs, beds, sewing machines, electric irons, etc., and also cleaning out the water towers. One of the jobs involved re-wiring the lights in the maternity ward. It seemed strange at first to wander in and out of the ward while babies were being born, mothers examined and nurses carried on tests, but nobody seemed to mind. One of the highlights of the trip was when I was allowed to watch an hour-long operation on a woman. The doctor described everything as he went along so it was most educational. I was a bit doubtful as to what my reactions would be seeing someone cut open, but I didn't faint, nor was I sick, although I took particular notice as to where the sinks were situated!

Dick and Phil went together to be instructors in a Trade Training Centre in the Cameroons. At this time the Cameroons, a small country bordering on the east side of Nigeria, were still under British Trusteeship, but they were preparing for the referendum which would eventually take them out of the Commonwealth to join with the former French Cameroons, and there was some uneasiness about the political situation. The Cameroonians themselves, however, were a people of simplicity and friendliness and, in the event, there were no upheavals. However, a number of British troops had moved in to keep order in case of subversive activity.

Dick and Phil were both boys of strong religious faith: Dick, a Catholic from Vulcan Foundaries, Phil from Rolls Royce. They were quiet unobtrusive youngsters who found themselves facing situations of a good deal more responsibility than they had ever been accustomed to, and their duties ranged far outside the narrow limits of technical training. Dick wrote:

I am now teaching English to all the apprentices as well as maths, and next year I shall be giving lessons to three assistant instructors in training. These are the people who will eventually take over the jobs of the European instructors. I

STUDENT

have also acquired the job of butcher for the whole of the staff and this entails sharing out of half a cow about once a fortnight. As you may know one of my favourite pastimes was Rugby Union, so I thought it would be a good idea if I could get some of the students interested in the game. This I did, and we used to hold training sessions twice a week. Some of the boys were becoming quite proficient at the game so I got them a game against the army in which they shaped very well indeed, and I hope to continue next season. I still attend the prayer meetings, debating societies and scouts.

and later on:

On the morning I moved into the workshop the instructor was involved in a serious motor accident, an all too common thing in the Cameroons, in which he broke both of his legs. The outcome of the accident was that the instructor is now back in the U.K. receiving treatment and I am running the shop.

One of Phil's early jobs involved water supply. All over Africa the problem of water was a major one, and of great importance not only intrinsically but because it was also bound up with the spread of disease. A great many volunteers found themselves attempting to alter or improve the supplies to their school or mission, but few were so well qualified to do so as Phil.

One of my jobs here was 'water engineer' as the system of supplying water to the compound was hardly adequate. Two jobs I did have on it kept me busy for a while; the first was to supervise the laying of a new 12' 6" long and 6" diameter cast iron pipe in the hydram which works from the river. This wasn't too bad, but the Cameroonians are fairly slow and the particular job happened to be very urgent. The pipe was eventually laid after sweating for about eight hours in the hot sun. The same applied later when it was decided that 600' of ¾" diameter water pipe needed laying. This was an easier job, but the three days sweating in the sun didn't help a great deal. It is great fun working alongside these lads, because as soon as you start talking to them you fail to realise that there are two different races working and talking together as one.

Phil graduated to being assistant to the Warden of the Training

Centre, and on one occasion when the latter was away he took the full weight of Warden's duties. In a tropical country, where life rarely runs on ordered lines but is full of unexpected hazards and developments, this meant hard work.

I must say I did enjoy my job as Warden, for the period of time I was acting, even though it meant rising at 5.30 a.m. most mornings. On three occasions I had to take lads to the hospital during the evening with fever and high temperatures. I also had the responsibility of getting nine new boys settled in the Centre, handing out punishment for various offences to certain boys, making sure that they get their correct 'chop' (food) each day and generally being Father to them.

Ken, from Warrington, who went to Sarawak and worked in a remote community development scheme was one of the apprentices who found himself in a situation far removed from his industrial background. He was dealing with a society at the beginning of technical development and this, for him, meant divesting himself of many of the higher ranges of his skill and being prepared to work in a very simple, basic way. It also meant that his qualities as a person became more important than his talents as a technician.

Just how to start telling you how much I am enjoying working here I don't really know. Each day seems to bring fresh experiences which go hand in hand with the routine work, making life extremely interesting.

Since Christmas we have been busily building and renovating. The old dispensary has moved to a room over the school. A new classroom has also been built—complete with semi-presentable stage. In February we had twenty thousand rubber seeds from Malaya and these we have carefully cultivated. We now have a miniature jungle of rubber plants—row upon row of them demanding to be weeded out and fertilised. When they are ready for transplanting in December they will be given to local Dayaks under the government planting scheme.

I find the people fascinating, and despite their semi-primitive existence they are the most hospitable and friendly people I have ever met. They are a backward people but very ready to learn and very progressively minded. With schemes like this they are beginning to help themselves and it is wonderful to see the progress going on all round.

Food here has also been an experience. I have eaten snails, frogs, tortoise, wasp grubs, together with many weird kinds of jungle fruits—strangely enough most of them were enjoyable. To say that I am in good health would be an understatement. I am fitter and healthier than when I arrived, and nearly eight pounds heavier.

Girls

One of the first countries to be prepared to accept the services of girl volunteers was Kenya. The social problems thrown up by a rapidly changing society, particularily in the town of Nairobi, were immense, and, as always, there were too few people to help, too little money and not enough official recognition of the importance of social welfare. The Christian Council of Kenya, which sponsored a great deal of youth work going on under different Christian agencies, found itself faced by a need which far outran resources. In 1959 Bronwyn went out to the Y.W.C.A., the first girl to serve in Africa.

She was eighteen, small and sensible, free for a year before going on to Teacher Training College. Very shortly after she arrived she found herself flung into the midst of responsibility.

MOTHER AND CHILD

103

The Warden at the hostel where I have been living and working has had to go away for a few days to recover. I have had the job of being warden, planning meals, supervising work, cooking, etc. Fortunately she is well again now. The Warden, however, at Bahati hostel has now fallen ill, (Bahati is the hostel for African girls down in one of the locations) and tonight I am to move in there. The girls there do their own cooking and cleaning, etc., but I understand there are different problems to face such as turning out boy-friends at 10 o'clock and seeing that girls are on time, etc.

She did not confine herself to hostel activities and once she had found her feet and become accustomed to the way of life, she began to look outward.

I hope very shortly to do some rural work in and around some of the villages in the Reserve. The rural programme organiser is on leave at the moment, but I know of at least two villages that are simply crying out for an informal education group for their women folk. Men are beginning more and more to see the advantages of having educated wives and daughters and once we have the chiefs on our side everything is fine. There has been some talk of the improprieties of letting a girl into the Reserve alone, but fortunately we have an extremely trusted and intelligent African driver who could also act as interpreter.

She succeeded in getting one or two small groups going and learnt enough of the local language to talk simply to the women. Her letters were factual and without vivid description but the worth of what she had done was well described in the letter that came shortly before her departure asking that she be replaced — not by one but by two more volunteers.

Later on work for girls expanded outside the orbit of the Y.W.C.A. into community service schemes in the very poor districts of Nairobi where the problem of children who could not get places in school, or who would not stay there even if they could, was a major one. Sophie, who was a graduate, went to help here.

I am living in Eastleigh now, which is nice as many of the children from the nursery school and some of my women and girls drop in in the evenings. There is really an incredible mix-up of races in Eastleigh, every possible combination. The nursery school is now going strong. We have forty children, which is our legal limit. To begin with so many children came who ought to have been in school that I set up a kind of 'getting into school' agency.

The women and girls are also quite well established now. I started in January for three afternoons a week, sewing, etc., and now there are about thirty women and fifteen assorted girls – all the women are African. I am going to start literacy and English with them, by request, and we're going to try and get a Red Cross person to do First Aid. The real problem is that the two groups ought to be separate but I can't cope with them both doing different things.

When Sari went to Malaya she also was the first girl to serve in that country. She went to a school for blind children under a mission. At first it seemed that a lack of specialised training might prove a serious drawback, and, while we could not do anything about this, efforts were made to make it possible for Sari to visit various institutions for the blind in the short time before she left. In the event, however, these fears were not justified; the school had, in any case, only one teacher on its staff who had any special knowledge of working with the blind.

The school was in Penang, a most beautiful island city off the coast of Malaya. It was here also that Michael and Geoff worked in the orphanage, but Sari's school, in a fine old colonial house set among oleanders and flowering trees, contrasted strikingly with the ramshackle buildings that housed the two boys. These three volunteers formed a firm friendship. Sari was a girl who made friends everywhere, her simple kindly open nature made it easy to confide in her, and she looked after the boys, inviting them up to huge meals when she felt that overwork and austerity were wearing them away.

Not long after her arrival she wrote:

The beginning of next week I shall be taking over one of the kindergarten classes as one of the teachers is returning to Australia. There are ten in the class, and the average age is about seven years. The children are mostly Chinese, with three Malays. Their blindness does not prevent them all being very different from each other.

There is Ken Fook, a strange little boy. His mother is a rubber tapper and was fourteen years when he was born. His mother and step-father won't have anything to do with him. Ken Fook was left here, and when the Principal traced his mother the step-father didn't even know of his existence! Anything Ken Fook lays his hands on he tries to eat.

Zahara Bee, a little Malay girl, just giggles when you ask her a question. Faridah, who doesn't look blind, never uses the word 'I' but always 'Faridah does something.'

Where I think I shall be of use is doing things which the staff never have time to do, such as taking a child to the market to feel and smell things, I am teaching myself to read and write braille.

Later:

I am teaching them the braille letters and also their numbers on Taylor frames. The trained teacher of the blind is helping me a tremendous amount, showing me the best methods etc. I must admit there have been many times when I've felt that I was an utter failure as a teacher. When the whole class was in chaos and wouldn't listen to what I said I felt like running away! Yet I wouldn't change this job for anything.

Liz, in Kenya, had sometimes the same feeling of failure but she expressed it in a different way!

COOKING CLASS

The English classes are often a bit of a trial, for I think up some brilliant idea that I'm sure they'd be interested in, but I'm just greeted with an air of submission and an attitude of 'Oh, well, we've got to come to this class anyway.' I'm determined to get some sort of reaction though, even if it means standing on my head and singing Shakespeare to a Christmas carol tune!

The girls, no less than the boys, tackled the jobs they went out to do with spirit and enthusiasm, and they showed the same sense and responsibility. There was caution at first in asking for them, and an inclination on the part of overseas employers to place them safely in the capital, but gradually, as it became apparent that they were not going to mope, or on the other hand to run amok, the requests increased and the projects became more adventurous. Although they all travelled by air the girls too had their adventures. Perhaps Diana, who went to teach in the remote New Hebrides, had the most nerve-racked journey.

No one had gone to the New Hebrides before Diana and we were not even very certain where they were, or how one got there. It proved to be a complicated business involving a change of plane in Paris and stop-overs in Australia and several of the smaller islands. Diana was due to leave on a Monday morning and she was coming down on Saturday to spend the week-end with us before she left. On the Wednesday her ticket, an expensive and complex document, was sent, registered, to Diana in Sheffield so that she should have the satisfaction of knowing herself fully prepared.

Diana arrived on Saturday evening in London and the first question we asked her was whether she had received the ticket.

'Ticket?' she said, 'What ticket?'

In the horrified silence there was recognition on both sides of the chaos that must now lie before us. Diana, it emerged, had gone on holiday with her family for the last week before leaving home — a fact which she had failed to pass on to us. She had, naturally, presumed that all last minute arrangements would be settled when she saw us at the week-end.

She rang up her father, who was in Nottingham, and he said he would drive back at once to Sheffield and retrieve the letter, then he would drive down to London with it. For a moment it seemed that all would be well. Not, however, for long. We remembered, suddenly, that the letter was registered and that, if the house was empty, it would not therefore be delivered. This was Saturday evening and the post office would be already closed.

Much later Diana's father phoned to tell us what we already knew, that the letter was not there and that the Post Office could not release it before 6 a.m. on Monday morning. Diana's mother would collect it at that time and take the first train down to London, then direct to London Airport, hoping to arrive before the plane left at 10 a.m.

We tried all the Sunday to pretend for Diana's sake, that all was well. She was eighteen and going alone to a most remote part of the world, we did not want her to leave in a state of turmoil if it could be helped. I do not know how far we succeeded: perhaps Diana, too, put a brave face on to comfort us! But on Sunday evening I knew that we could not depend on the arrival of her ticket and that first thing on Monday morning we must take steps to replace it.

Very early on Monday Diana and I arrived at the Air Terminal and explained to a sympathetic hostess the dilemma in which we found ourselves. Unless she caught the 10 a.m. plane to Paris all connections would be lost and she would have to wait a week.

The hostess was charming, but action could only be taken at the airport itself. They put us on an early bus and sent us out there to see the Air France officials. In turn they, too, were charming, but replacing a ticket of this kind, and of this expense, was not a simple matter that could be done on the spur of the moment. Could I guarantee that the first ticket was, in fact, on its way to London and would be handed in? Where had it been bought? Was it paid for and by whom? Some complicated telephone calls then ensued and, whether because the results were satisfactory, or whether because Diana had begun to look rather forlorn, we were told that they would make us out another ticket.

This was the first hurdle over but there was still some way to go. I had innocently imagined that it would be easy to write out a second piece of paper, but it was not so. There were lists to be consulted, stages to be checked, finance to be worked out. While we waited the loudspeaker announced the first, second, and at last the final, call for the 10 a.m. Air France plane. When this happened the stewardess turned from her labours at the desk and said casually to a friend:

'Go down and tell that Captain he is not to take off until this passenger is on board.'

I knew then that we were safe, and while we waited the next few, interminable minutes I savoured the experience of having an aeroplane kept waiting for me, while poor Diana gazed anxiously towards the stairs hoping to see her mother arriving after all.

Eventually it was done and we were hurried through the Customs hall and the outer corridors right down to the plane itself. Diana, by now pale and shaking, was bundled on board and I returned to wait for her mother in the booking hall. She arrived a few minutes later, very nearly in tears, her only thought that she had not arrived in time for her daughter to catch the plane. When I told her that we had, in fact, managed to get her on board and we had handed the extra ticket over to our friend the stewardess, we both retired to the buffet to drink coffee and recover.

Two weeks later a letter arrived from Diana, safely landed in the New Hebrides. She was acting as Deputy to the Headmistress of a girls' boarding school, active and happy, and already fast becoming expert at the favourite local sport—football played with bare feet!

FILIPINO BOY

CHAPTER III

Extra Activities

YOUNG DAYAK

Music and Drama

ANGUS, who went to the Solomon Islands, was a large, red-haired Scot, who worried in the weeks before he left about his glass of fresh milk every day. Would he be able to continue to have it? When assured that it was most unlikely, Angus shrugged and set himself to believe that he could survive without fresh milk. For eighteen years he had never had to and this one change in his way of life seemed to sum up for him all the strangeness and uncertainty that he was letting himself in for.

However Angus was a lad who, while he took life seriously, did not make heavy weather of living. Robust, cheerful, forthright, he was prepared to try anything, and determined to make a success of everything. He did not always do so, but he continued to try.

He went to teach with a mission in the Solomon Islands and threw himself without reserve into the multiplicity of extra activities which were often the real crown of the volunteer's year. It was on the job undertaken after four o'clock, or at the week-end, the work

110

which was not only the volunteer's project but also his pleasure, that friendships were made and understanding gained; and it was in trying to help with these activities, which so frequently concerned the things which lay nearest his own heart, that the volunteer came to recognise some of the real difficulties of communication between people and to discover in himself depths that he had not previously suspected he possessed.

Angus was musical. He wrote:

> One of my biggest activities here is choral work. I have three different choirs which I have to keep supplied with material. To meet the demand I've had to write harmony and arrange myself. I think I'll have enough to last me until I leave for home. My next big piece is to be 'O Thou that Tellest Good Tidings to Zion'. I hope it doesn't prove too difficult.

But, alas, it did.

> I'm sorry to tell you that 'O Thou that Tellest Good Tidings to Zion' had to be given up. These people have an incurable habit of dropping pitch very quickly. Thus any singing they do they have to start very high in order not to be too low at the end the song.

Music could be a potent creative factor in bringing people together. Particularly in Africa was this true, where the musical idiom was understandable in European terms, and many volunteers found themselves moved by the singing of their pupils. In Tanganyika Robin, teaching in a mission school far removed from any urban centre, was involved in the whole gamut of musical appreciation.

> I teach all the school's music, which is mostly singing, though I am trying to bring in variations. There is really no adequate keyboard instrument here, though I am scheming for a piano somehow. There is, however, a gramophone, which will make the task easier. I find the music difficult myself as all the services are in Swahili and I have to sing hymns in this, and at the same time read the music in Tonic Sol-fa, an abomination I am hoping to crush. As yet the boys know little of European music, and I hope to get that right, too. I think this is almost as important as learning to speak English.

There are some people who contest the teaching of European

music to Africans, and I'd perhaps better justify my case. In the first place African music is scarce and not usually written. Its associations to Africans make it generally undesirable in church music, which is after all the only music for most, though the small amount used is very worthy. In the second place they are really keen to listen to and appreciate European music, as I have already found. The Bishop brought us a record of an African choir of Johannesburg singing the 'Messiah' which I have used in senior-form lessons, and I passed round my score, which I squeezed into my forty-four pounds. They loved it and asked for more. I have already got one pupil on the small Dulatone keyboard instrument operating on tuning forks (which I have had to refit). I have started a choir and there are some exceptional voices here.

He was not content, however, to accept what he found on the spot as unalterable.

I'm on the road to rectifying the musical situation after begging an organ of the foot-bellows type from the mission at Lindi, and persuading our Indian agent to take it to Masasi free of charge,

then bringing it up here in the Land Rover. I had to make a new set of bellows out of borrowed material, and with tacks, glue, sacking and a few well-aimed blows, it now works with a most enjoyable tone.

Drama, too, in many different forms was inevitably an activity in which volunteers working in schools became engaged sooner or later. Very often a harrassed headmaster was only too glad to hand over the school play to his latest young recruit! In Africa, although most

SCHOOL BAND

pupils had a strong aversion to rehearsing and disliked any form of disciplined preparation, they were extremely talented impromptu actors, capable of turning out a splendid performance on the night, however disastrous the dress rehearsal might have been. Far Eastern peoples, on the whole less extrovert, did not have quite this same facility. But for them, too, drama could be a liberating experience.

In Sarawak Keith was immersed in the perennial school concert.

The next couple of weeks were the last of term, and they brought with them the much-heralded school concert. I was struggling desperately to keep my motley crew of players on their toes. We had splendid costumes of vividly-coloured crepe paper which they loved, and we even managed to make a set out of jungle wood, paint and paper. On the big night everything went perfectly, and the audience laughed so much that we were forced to pause from time to time until the din subsided. The boys are as keen as mustard to do another one, and I am now trying to encourage the Iban teachers to learn how to produce a play so that they can take over when we leave.

Underlining all activities was the theme of 'when we leave'. The volunteers were very aware of the temporary nature of their role and of their position as 'outsiders', and perhaps the most difficult of all their tasks was the stimulating of an interest among the local personalities which would eventually render a volunteer unnecessary in that situation. It was also their most important function, and they well knew that success or failure was not to be measured immediately, but in what grew from the seeds they planted in the years after they had gone. For youngsters this was a difficult truth to accept; it is in the nature of youth to wish to see immediate results and to take credit for them. But most volunteers showed themselves fully capable of seeing their year in its true perspective and recognising wherein its value was likely to lie — both for themselves and those they served.

Sean, in North Borneo, trying to help his young Chinese pupils in their difficulties with the English language, turned to drama for assistance.

The mock trial was great fun. I utilised all my clothing for the costumes. I do not think even the characters understood the course of the trial completely, but the quite large audience enjoyed it because of the costumes and the slapstick comedy, which I introduced in large doses in order to make it interesting—even if it was incomprehensible. The fat smiling boy in the sarong was a natural comic, and the venerable judge (myself) had to control himself while this witness gave evidence. It was all done with due formality (we had a clerk of the court and swearing in, etc.): I wrote out the questions for the two lawyers as they could not be expected to do it themselves and they read them. But the witnesses had to answer without papers. I really enjoyed it and I think they did, too.

ROMAN SOLDIER

I have now started an acting club and shall have to get down to writing a short play for them soon. I don't know how I will do it. The birth pangs of the trial composition were laboured enough.

And, of course, there was always Shakespeare. All over the world, sooner or later, the school embarked on a production of *The Merchant of Venice* or *A Midsummer Night's Dream,* and small black Portias or coffee-coloured Ariels lent their own special flavour to scenes whose background was very far removed from anything they, or their audience, could have remotely imagined. In Aden it was *Julius Caesar,* and Michael, intelligent and faintly sardonic, was torn between his strong sense of the ridiculous and a real affection for his pupils.

To come to more recent times. I am deep in the blood of Julius Caesar. We are battling desperately to preserve Shakespeare from utter ruin, and time alone will tell how we have fared. To hear some of the pint-sized, squeaky-voiced Indian kids saying, 'Hail Sheezer, read thish schedule' with about as much expression as a disinterested vacuum cleaner salesman is enough to give a cat hysterics. For the rest, trying to push them into something, being exasperated by their lack of oomph, bite, spine, infuriated by their softened outlook, disarmed by their laissez faire attitude, conquered by their eagerness.

114

Aden was not an easy place to work; a barren, rocky, coastal strip, battered by a ferocious climate, and Michael's final sentence summed up well some of the difficulties in human relations.

Projects

The group of volunteers who worked in Aden were all concerned with teaching in a secondary school in Aden itself. They worked with a difficult, sophisticated elite, the sons of rich parents, a privileged minority—but with no tradition of noblesse oblige. The country itself was harsh and hot, with an atmosphere of cynicism and intrigue which was enhanced, rather than counterbalanced, by the cosmopolitan surroundings of a large naval base.

In this environment extra-curricular activities, which were recognised by the volunteers to be important, were difficult to encourage. There was no real keenness over sports, clubs were poorly and intermittently attended, and, in general, the idea of doing more than the bare minimum of either work or play was considered curious. One or two of the volunteers went down in the evenings to help with a Jewish boys' club for a time, though the two who wished to help a misssion were told that they must not do so. And the prospect of the school holidays, when in other parts of the world volunteers were undertaking extensive and exciting expeditions in the company of their pupils, was, in Aden, a depressing one.

One January, on his way back from the Far East, my husband had some hours in Aden, and he met with Ted and Peter and Roger and Robert, and with some of their students. My husband had given some thought to the difficulties and disillusionments consequent on working in this part of the world, and he was determined to try to spark, with the volunteers, some ideas of community service. I think it is probable that before his arrival Ted and the others would have said this was not possible, nevertheless, to their surprise and admiration, he succeeded—and he left them to fan into flame the small fire that he had started burning.

The boys, to whom you had suggested a work camp, were so keen on the idea that they wanted to start straight away and do something during this coming holiday. Their suggestion is to go to

115

some area where the cotton crop is abundant, but where there is neither enough money or labour to pick it all.

So wrote Roger some weeks later; and then Ted described how the plans were developing.

Robert has been doing sterling work finding 'contacts' for our cotton-picking in the Protectorate next holidays. There is much enthusiasm for the scheme especially amongst the boys to whom the idea is completely new. Normally manual work is reserved for the sweepers, slaves and uneducated types. Also the Arab is very individualistic and the fact that we have got the boys to agree to do manual work together is a major triumph.

There were, of course, checks and snags. It was not easy to take a party into the hinterland of Aden, the part known as the Protectorate, where life was still full of tribal feuds and there was a good deal of official nervousness about both 'safety' and 'subversion'. However the volunteers worked steadily towards the goal, and eventually they succeeded. They not only got into the Protectorate, they also managed to present the whole endeavour in such a way that it ended up as a small landmark in the social history of Aden.

You will, I am sure, be pleased to hear that the cotton-picking scheme in the Protectorate was a great success. In addition to the four of us we took one Arab master and fifteen boys, all boarders. We had an escort from the Federal National Guard, who provided free transport, and we stayed in a school in Mudia. We did not do as much work as *we* had planned—three to four hours a day, but it was more than they expected, and we definitely helped the poor farmers (some of whom are really poor). The hospitality was magnificent.

It was a raving success and the farmers were obviously pleased. In the evenings the whole contingent was asked out to some feast or other. It was great fun. From my point of view I learned a lot about the Protectorate Arab to admire and respect. From the boys point of view it probably did them even more good. They learnt to work together instead of 'sitting in their own country' doing nothing.

So reported Peter and Ted.
Work camps of this kind were not unknown in other parts of the

CONSTRUCTION WORK

world, and were a good deal easier to organise — though they too had their snags. The Aden project had been fortunate in its actual task of cotton-picking, which was obviously of genuine worth and importance, but finding a job which fulfilled a real need was not always easy and in India the Johns ran into snags.

A request for the services of two volunteers had come from a Rural Life Centre in Southern India, and, at first sight, it appeared to lay down some impossible conditions. They wished to have a boy who spoke either Tamil or Malayalam, knew about artifical insemination and tropical diseases in cattle and fowls, and was expert in non-equipment games! When we read it, and then thought of our school-leavers, we sat back and laughed.

However, by a strange coincidence, at the very next selection

117

board there appeared two candidates, one of whom had spent some of his early life in India and had then spoken Malayalam, the other, whose parents worked in Hong Kong, wanted to be a vet. Both were called John. Further research revealed that John No. 1's father had been a missionary in the area from which the request came, and that John No. 2 wanted to spend his summer holidays in Hong Kong before going on to his assignment. Some hard work then made it possible for him to attend the Hong Kong Veterinary Department during his vacation to learn all he could about artificial insemination and tropical diseases, so that when he and John No. 1 met in Madras at the end of September we had, in fact, gone some distance towards filling the conditions required of us. The situation was, however, even further complicated by the fact that the pastor in charge of the centre was also called John, and the resultant confusion sometimes made correspondence very difficult to sort out.

In the event the Johns' project proved a difficult one, vague and undefined, and the skills which we had so laboriously produced in them went virtually unused, though for a long time they incubated chickens in their bedroom; but the extra-mural activities which they managed from time to time to set up proved enjoyable and interesting.

Our four days work camp with the boys was quite successful. I say quite, because it turned out that what road we built was only of use to the 'caste' village, whereas it was a Christian village for which we were supposed to be working. The Headmaster, who is a caste Hindu, was apparently trying to get into the good books of this caste village by getting us to use our time for them. However the work was good and we are going again in April to finish the road to the other village.

We slept in one quite small schoolroom with the sixty boys and six masters. Talk about living under a microscope twenty-four hours a day! The first night we didn't sleep a wink, but we got used to the rope cots which were at least two feet too short. The first night, actually, we slept on the floor as the boys did, but then we decided that discretion was the better part of valour, luckily there were no mosquitos so we didn't have to shame ourselves by using nets. We slept in dohties (an Indian cloth), swam in a well, and sang everything we could remember from 'Baa, Baa Black Sheep', 'Twinkle, Twinkle Little Star', 'Jack and Jill', to the latest pop tunes. Taught them a couple of team games in what spare time there was. In fact we had a thoroughly enjoyable time.

A large part of the school holidays, in many parts of the world, was occupied in constructional and maintenance activities, and the form that these took was surprisingly constant. In Sarawak latrines, fish-ponds and drains were high priority, and almost everywhere in Africa and Asia the volunteer sooner or later found himself wrestling with the water supply. In Southern Rhodesia and Tanganyika two Roberts successfully repaired pumping engines, and ended up in charge of plumbing and mechanics: in the Solomons Roger helped with the construction of a sick-bay, which was really a disused garage manhandled to a different site, and in Sarawak the building of teachers' houses was commonplace. Robin, who discovered a talent for engineering when he managed to resurrect two aged petrol engines, wrote from Tanganyika:

I've learnt an immense amount from being here doing jobs that I'd never have done in England because I'd never had the training. I'd have gone on calling in an engineer to do all the servicing, and have continued to take the car to the garage every time something went wrong. Now that I've got our piano here and installed I've had to learn to tune it myself too. I suppose when I get home I shall go back to my old ways in many things including garages, but I shall never forget the experience I've had here.

There was even an enterprising boy in Nigeria who started snail farming, 'which seems a useful and cheap way of getting meat!', but I doubt if this idea had a very long life. And a girl in Kenya bred rabbits and reared chickens to help out the very tight budget of the mission with which she worked. One activity surprised the volunteers who found themselves engaged in it. From Jamaica Charlie wrote:

Although I am too young to vote I was considered old enough to be a Presiding Officer at the Local Government Election in March. It was fascinating. You still have to explain to most people what to do. Everyone has to dip their finger in a red ink to prevent double voting. I had only two people with grease on their fingers to prevent the ink from staining so they could vote again. The officer at the next table knocked her bottle over, so gallantly I mopped it up for her. My hands were stained red for months after.

Across the world, in Somaliland, Peter and David found themselves coping with a very similar situation.

We had the most welcome opportunity of participating in the Protectorate's first General Election. We were rather surprised to hear the Assistant Director of Education suggest that two nineteen-year-olds were going to be in charge of a polling station when the minimum age for voting was twenty-one. Boys who were obviously as young as fifteen or sixteen did not protest further as to their not being able to vote when they were informed that their presiding officer was only nineteen.

Here, too, fingers were dipped in ink to prevent duplication of votes. Peter and David, having assisted at this first stage in the achieving of independence, were later to see its full development and to be the first two volunteers to start work in a country which was a British Protectorate and end up working in that same country now a fully independent, non-Commonwealth nation.

Occasionally too there were civic duties of a more dramatic kind. Warren was one of the volunteers working with youth clubs in Kenya. He was an apprentice from the Midlands, stocky, tough, blunt, and he found himself up-country organising a club for some hundreds of youngsters. He, too, did his share at the polling booth; he also helped authority when the need arose.

On returning back home I just got time to take my boots off when the District Officer came back to say he'd just received a signal to say that a lorry had overturned with twenty people on

BUILDING A NEW MARKET

board, and would I help him. We took three Land Rovers and sent all the wounded off to hospital, then we were left to do the dirty work. We put six dead bodies in the back of my car and then drove to the police station. The District Officer was feeling sickly by the time we got home. I was lucky that it didn't affect me.

Sport

Sports formed a major out-of-school activity, and it was perhaps not surprising that it was often on the sports field that many problems of attitude came sharply into focus. A youngster from Britain, whatever his personal feelings about games, once outside his own country found himself strongly in favour of certain accepted ideas on the sports field. It was a shock to him to discover that these ideas were not necessarily shared by those with whom he was working. The object of a match was to win it, on the face of it a common and admirable aim, but even this simple goal was surrounded by complications. Fred, in North Borneo, wrestling with his Chinese pupils' introversion, arranged a tour for the football team that he had, with much effort, been nursing. The result was another discouragement for him.

I told you about the football tour. This was a fine example of the difference between Eastern and Western concepts and attitudes to life. I took a party of fifteen boys to Jesselton, consisting of both 1st Team players and 2nd Team players. We were scheduled to play three games, and I was determined that every boy should have at least one game. For the first match I had the 1st Team centre-half playing at left-back. We lost 0 – 6. I was told in no uncertain terms that it was a disgrace for a Chinese to lose and that they had therefore lost face. I pointed out that in my opinion it did not matter what the result was as long as the team tried their best, but the remark fell upon stony ground. It was pointed out to me that there were great differences between East and West and this was one of them.

Fred came home at the end of his year feeling that he had made little impression on the school at Tenom. But the ground was not so stony as he had imagined and the seeds he sowed bore fruit, although he was not there to see the results. A year later his successor was able to write about the same school:

LAND DAYAK
FOOTBALL MATCH

One especially good thing that happened here was a football match a day or so ago which the school 'A' team played with the Public Works Department workers. We lost 0 − 1, but played outstandingly well against a strong, tough, big, experienced team. The game was without any rough or foul play whatever. The boys said they enjoyed it more than most games. I think the standard of the game was mainly due to the exemplary keenness and cleanness of the Timorese and Dusun opponents, but I could pat myself on the back lightly for encouraging the boys to practise more (they're not keen on training), giving them a few general hints, and stamping out rough play and rule evasion − I had to make sure of the rules myself first!

He could also have patted Fred on the back for taking the strain in the early days when it was felt that any defeat, however honourable, was something not to be tolerated.

122

Meanwhile Sean, in the same school, concentrated on his speciality — gymnastics.

> The gym is done by my most junior section, who are also the most keen and have come on in a rush lately. I enjoy them very very much. We are a trifle hampered by the lack of more than a small mat and of a box also. I use my desk for a box and cover it with a mat, but this has many snags: (1) it is too wide; (2) it is too high; (3) it is unsteady; (4) if I use the mat on it, which I have to, they have nothing soft to land on.

This activity, however, also had its snags. It was very difficult to get the boys to do any practice at all on their own, and Sean was continually exasperated by the fact that the older boys were constantly deserting him to put in yet another extra hour with their books.

In Sarawak Ian's talents lay in rugby football rather than soccer, but he turned this to his advantage by being prepared to let his pupils teach him the subtleties of playing with a round ball. He was still conscious of his great height, but now found that this could be an asset also.

> I have been playing a lot of football and basketball with the boys. My ability in both games has improved a lot, and being the tallest person in the school (probably in the town as well), I have a natural advantage in basketball, which I use to the full whenever I think my prestige (not very great) has taken a beating by a five-footer running round me. The rugby is not very popular yet. Some of them will play so fanatically that they put the rest off by thumping them hard. The idea of passing as anything but a last resort is foreign to the Iban mind, and some of them get their elbows working like sword-edged pistons in order not to have to stop and pass: one of my local rules is that you must pass once you have stopped running!

Towards the middle of his year a Big Walk was organised by the local community, and this Ian entered for. This activity seemed to be a popular one in the Borneo territories and consisted of a mammoth mass walk covering a considerable distance and ending up all round the town. It was the first time that a European had entered for this event, and Ian, long legs flailing and red hair flaming, was very conspicuous. He came in among the first dozen but the place he took was not really important; all along the route and in the streets of the little town the people crowded to the doors of their huts and houses to watch this young giant striding by, prepared to pit his skill on equal terms with the local people and to lose the race cheerfully.

It was not unusual for a volunteer to be the only representative of his people in a team. For one thing he was now working in countries where the British were very much in a minority. Sometimes, however, it assumed rather more importance because it was a deliberate step across a clear-cut barrier. In Nyasaland Ron reported:

> We rather pride ourselves on being the first Europeans to play in an African soccer team. Quite a few eyes were opened on that occasion, and we like to think that we are setting some precedents for ourselves and others.

In the terms of race relations in Nyasaland at this time this was a real gesture, not on the part of Ron, to whom it was the natural thing to do, but on the part of the African team which issued the invitation to him to play for them. There was a lighter side to it too. Many footballers in Africa and elsewhere played barefoot and this, at first a shock to the British boy, often became accepted practice for him as well as for them. David wrote from the Solomons:

> By the end of last week I had conquered barefoot football, though it was rather a painful process.

Clubs

The encouraging of extra-curricular clubs of all kinds, or the support of already existing clubs, was something that concerned all volunteers working in schools. In this case clubs were a secondary activity — unlike the full-time projects in youth work — and there were many advantages in a close relationship with the school. It could, for instance, help to have a 'captive' audience, who could be persuaded, or bribed, into membership.

BOXING

In North Borneo it was the official policy of the Education Department to encourage the volunteers, all of whom served in a teaching capacity in schools, to put their spare-time energies into clubs. There was no doubt in the mind of the Director of Education that the contribution made out of school in this way was just as great as the contribution made actually in the classroom.

Nevertheless, in spite of official recognition and backing, this particular job was not an easy one. Among the Chinese societies of all kinds played a large part in social life, but one of their distinguishing features was that they were exclusive, tight-knit, closed groups formed to further some purpose, political, social or economic. For them, as perhaps to a lesser extent for their Malay fellow citizens, the idea of an open youth club, one of the objects of which would be to make contact with those of other races, was a strange one. When that youth club also attempted to mix the sexes as well as the races the complications became overwhelming. In a sense the volunteers had a great deal against them in this endeavour because, although a youth club had existed in Jesselton, the capital, long before any volunteers arrived there, the need for it was felt more by those in authority than by the potential members; and to rouse enthusiasm as well as to organise and create the actual structure was a formidable task.

Richard, who worked at a secondary school in the capital, bore a considerable amount of the burden of the youth club.

We are going to get the school musicians to practice hard and then we will get them to play at the youth club. If this is a success we thought we could move on to the large community centre, where we would hold a concert sometime after Christmas. We thought that a number of songs with choruses could be included in the programme in order to get the audience to sing—as far as we know this is not done here. The visit of the band, and we hope a small choir, to the youth club will not only encourage our musicians but also enliven the moribund state of affairs at the youth club. It is rather difficult for us to do anything to pep it up at present as there is something sadly amiss with the committee, with whom we cannot get in touch, and without whose consent it would be foolish and unwise of us to meddle in its affairs.

Later:

The youth club, which has defeated us for six months, looks

more hopeful now. I have just been co-opted on to the members' committee and so now will have more say in what goes on. Previously we have supplied them with numerous ideas, which they have tried to put into effect with very little success. The roots of the trouble are two-fold. One is the extreme conservatism of the Chinese: the boys are shy or afraid of girls and won't ask them to dances or to their meetings, and the girls who are asked have to fight hard to obtain parental approval before they can go out with their boy friends.

The second difficulty is to interest the indigenous youth. This is peculiarily difficult as it is almost impossible to get the adults, let alone the youth, to take an active interest in their country. The local population is fearfully complacent and does nothing to further its own interest, and few join voluntary associations.

Later:

To start with I have some good news. At long last the youth club is awakening form its long sleep. We have a new youth leader, an Indian master at the government secondary school. He is showing great interest and has got things moving. I am in charge of the social evenings, cycling and life saving departments. The social evenings are most encouraging. The first one was on Commonwealth Youth Sunday and we had an attendance of over eighty, including ten girls whom we had arranged to come complete with chaperone.

Later:

The youth club management committee have finally passed the measure allowing girls to become members, so there is plenty of scope for the two new girl volunteers there. If they could persuade the girls to push the boys around a bit a lot of good would come of it.

In due course the girls arrived, Diana and Denise, the first two girls to serve in North Borneo. They threw themselves at once into the activities and problems of the Youth Club. Not very long after they had arrived Diana wrote:

Last Tuesday we held a meeting for all the girls who were interested to elect a committee for the girls' section of the youth club. The meeting was poorly attended despite much publicity, but we were able to elect four members to the committee. Denise had previously been appointed girls' youth leader, and I am now secretary of the committee. As a beginning we have formed sections for basketball, hockey, swimming and cycling, and — when we have the huge membership we are determined to get — we hope to start other sections, such as dancing, drama, badminton, etc.

Alas, however, these sanguine hopes were not realised and much later Denise wrote:

The girls' youth club is a failure. I think there is insufficient need for a girls' club yet — too many girls are content to stay at home and resent being expected to join youth club activities. We are hoping to hold the few interested girls together with occasional outings, but I think there is little that we can do to increase interest and membership.

The main trouble is that the idea of regular activities seems foreign to the young people here, and the girls in particular would prefer on the whole to do nothing than to do something. Oddly enough everyone here (including the youngsters at the club) thinks the club is flourishing, and Diana and I are the only ones who realise that it exists in name only.

The situation, however, was not always quite so gloomy. Oliver, who worked with Richard in Jesselton, was fortunate in having a talent of his own sufficiently self-consuming to attract others to him. He was a good artist, and he started an art club which successfully survived his own departure a year later. He organised an exhibition with considerable local publicity, gave lessons, and took classes out on sketching expeditions to the great interest of the village children. He was helped in this by the naturally artistic bent of the Malays, and had the satisfaction of knowing that the thing he most enjoyed doing was greatly appreciated locally.

It was not only in the capital that difficulties arose. In a small seaport town on the north coast of North Borneo the volunteers also wrestled with the problems of a youth club in their spare time from teaching in a mission school.

Always before you is the suspicion and sometimes ill-feeling of Chinese to Malay and vice-versa. The youth club does a lot of good in trying to mix them up. I want to have a go at discussion groups and perhaps debates (big language problem here). Dances are out (immoral) and there are many difficulties before both races begin to mix freely with each other.

Up in Tenom Sean and Fred were, perhaps, less ambitious. They confined their activities to the school, and attempted to create clubs among their pupils which would help them, indirectly, with their academic work. Even this, however, had its depressing moments. Sean wrote:

This is where the greatest challenge lies. If we wished we could easily sit back and do nothing. However neither of us want to see them or us stagnate in an aura of study.

Periodically we have moods of profound depression when it does not seem as if we are making any progress at all. The stamp club, which has quite a large following, has meetings about once a week; it is kept interested by the fact that the meetings are short and by the stamps which are given out at the beginning each time.

My newest venture has not yet had its inauguration so I cannot tell you how it is going. It is just a general English-speaking club for the seniors. In it I am going to have talks and lectures and certain projects. One of them is to make a guide-book of Tenom, and another, very shadowy one at the moment, is to get them to find out all they can about Tenom in the Jap occupation and write a report on it.

Undoubtedly clubs were a struggle, involving most volunteers in far-ranging problems of how to arouse and sustain interest, even of the usefulness of clubs at all. But this was a problem not confined to overseas, a fact that was often consoling in moments of depression, and in tackling and thinking about these difficulties some volunteers were laying the foundations for a later concern about exactly the same perplexities in their own country.

Scouts, Boys' Brigade, etc.

The request from Somaliland, which was eventually answered by Peter and David, had specifically asked that one, at least, of the volunteers should be a Scout. So Peter, who was a Queen's Scout, went out with the special object of helping to organise and encourage Scouting in the territory. David had never been a Scout, but the friendship and sympathy which developed between these two

SCOUTS

volunteers was so genuine that he very soon found himself drawn into Peter's enthusiasm, and, as in everything else, they shared completely the trials and triumphs of their year overseas. Peter wrote at some length of the work with the Scouts.

When I arrived the headmaster of my school had been running a Scout troop for a year. I was almost immediately involved. Since then we have doubled the size of the troop (fourteen to twenty-eight), and have a waiting-list of seventy-five boys alone ... and at least three other towns are crying out for instruction and assistance in starting troops. Also there is a mixed Cub pack (the Scouts are all Somali for there are no European teenagers) with which I help, and also a Brownie pack (European), but as yet I have not ventured there. I'm afraid I could not sit around a toadstool listening to Wise Old Owl!

We went out with the Scouts for a night hike soon after we arrived. We ate their food, much to their delight, which consisted of onions and tomatoes fried in ghee, a kind of fat, to which is added washed rice and boiling water and the whole left to cook. Meat is added if available. We got a very big shock when we saw how big four ounces of cooked rice really was. The first meal was rather difficult to accept, but since then I have become accustomed to it and would go so far as to say I could appreciate it.

The presence of two British boys who actually camped with them and could walk as far and as fast as they did (apparently many Somali boys were under the impression that Europeans were almost incapable of walking at all, because they rarely saw them out of motor-cars) acted as a tremendous fillip to the Scout movement in Somaliland, as it then was. So many of their pupils were eager to join that Peter and David were forced to resort to pulling the names out of a hat, and any privacy they might have had was now shattered by the crowds of small boys who arrived to knock on their door and demand to join the Scouts.

Peter described two trips made with the Scout troop.

129

The trip to Berbera was by three-ton truck. The whole of the hundred and ten miles is just a track with many miles of corrugation. We travelled in the back of a lorry together with twenty scouts, luggage and food; quite an experience I can assure you. In Berbera we played the town football team. I played, but my efforts were not very rewarding for football is popular here and the Somalis are very good. However my attempts, and especially my failure, were delightfully received by the crowd who laughed loud and long.

After the game as we returned to the truck the usual few stones came flying towards me from the young boys. Somalis seem to revel in stonethrowing, they throw them at everything from camels and goats to much less inanimate objects, to David and me, and even each other. However this particular show was greatly disapproved of by the Scouts and our driver. One of the scouts leapt from the lorry, caught one of the boys and gave him a really good hiding (also in typical Somali tradition and much to the delight of the crowd) while the driver was so annoyed at this insult that he chased one small boy in two complete close circles with the three-ton truck! I might say he nearly got the boy in question, and he certainly terrified him.

We also went fishing, the first time for all the boys and I am sorry to say they were all very disillusioned and disappointed when we did not catch anything. They seemed to think the fish just came along to be caught, and all of them believed one threw the hooks at the fish and hoped they stuck in them!

I am proud to announce that we are now officially recognised by I.H.Q. London. We now have our own name-tape, 1st Hargeisa, we have designed our own Somaliland badge which we hope to have woven soon, and we are indicated on the map of 'Scouting in the Commonwealth' in this year's Scout Diary.

In another Moslem country, lying across a narrow strip of sea, another Peter also spent much of his spare time on Scouts. In Aden, however, the situation was rather different and there was none of the enthusiasm that made the task in Somaliland so enjoyable in spite of its occasional surprises. In Aden the taboos of a society built upon complete male domination complicated the most innocent of actions, and Peter, concerned to adapt Scouting to the country which he found so little suitable for the traditional British ploys of camping, fire-lighting, building huts and dens, had his best-laid plans bedevilled by suspicions.

The camps we had and the excursions we pursued soon sorted out the sheep from the goats, and our numbers, though chosen as carefully as we could, were soon halved. I found that those who were prepared to try enjoyed themselves and are still Scouts, while those who had given up before they had even tried an exercise out soon left.

We have had a camp in the gardens, which are very good for camps and the resulting hunt for natural and unnatural things, and the only place where there are a few trees for climbing and rope ladders. But it was still a little artificial for people going to live their entire lives in Aden, so we have another place, where we only used those things that one might find anywhere.

We slept in an old derelict house, and this was set on the top of a high cliff. At one time someone set themselves the laborious task of building steps down the sheer face of this cliff. Hardly anyone knows of these steps, but they lead down to a perfect place for both watching and catching fish of the most rare and extraordinary types, and we went down there in moonlight brighter than one ever sees it in England, and six people managed to catch one fish. We also managed to catch the lighthouse as it was lighting up, and though there was not very much to see, it was something new for them.

The following day I had decided to go as far round the coast as we could to the other side of the Colony. This has only ever been done successfully by two airmen, so I didn't expect to make it, and so well did the fellows know the reputation of impossibility that they were extremely reluctant to follow me. Having been dismayed at the first difficulty, they were extremely surprised to find that it was not, as they had thought, impossible; and once we were over that the spirit changed to a fantastic degree. We did not make the entire round, but did enough to make them say they had, all except one, enjoyed it immensely.

I thought it decidedly funny (peculiar) that having lived in this place all their lives, they take the place so for granted that it required someone from outside to come to show them the facilities for variety and occupations and interests that there are in such an apparently dull place. It is a very easy thing to climb the highest

131

mountain in the Colony, and yet none of them had ever done it before. They were immensely surprised at what fun it was to go on a really good walk. But there is a great deal of opposition not only from the lack of enthusiasm, which is a thing cured easily by time, but more from laziness, which often causes them not to turn up, and then there is little you can do.

But the most trouble comes from the parents who, though prepared to let the boy go once a week to the meeting just so that he is occupied, cannot fathom the enthusiasm of anyone who tries to organise a camp in which the boys sleep out, and proceed to attribute it to bad desires and will not allow the boys to go.

As in many other things, Aden was perhaps the most difficult territory in which to help Scouting. The rigid framework of Islam, combined with an increasing abandonment of the old religious values though still within that framework, made a situation which it was hard for a youngster from a totally different background to penetrate. The Aden Arab boys were a great deal more sophisticated in their view of the world than was Peter; but perhaps his innocent enthusiasm, which he had in full measure, enabled him to go as far towards creating an open friendly atmosphere as anyone could have done.

Elsewhere the pattern was more conventional, though with local variations which made for an interesting life. In the Solomon Islands John found himself facing a rather surprising challenge.

On arrival at the camping site the scouts built leaf shelters and other scouts caught fish. After church the local teacher from the near-by village told us in pidgin English that a 'vela' or spirit had haunted the village the previous night and the villagers were relying on the scouts to drive it away. Whether this was the reason for the gifts of many baskets of yams, kumara and pana I have yet to discover!

CLIMBING

Neither did we discover: the success or failure of the Scouts with the 'vela' had been forgotten by the time the next letter arrived.

It could, however, happen that it was the volunteer who caused the stir, and not the strangeness or eccentricity of local custom. William, an extremely able boy whose gifts were primarily academic, went to Western Nigeria. The school to which he was allocated had asked for someone to teach Latin and play the organ, and it so happened that William was competent to do both. However he was also briefed that he should make himself as proficient in sports as he could. Nigerians enjoying all kinds of games and, particularly in this region, boxing. William took this seriously, and, while never very brilliant himself, he encouraged and participated in all kinds of outdoor activities.

On arrival at the school he found that the Scout troop lacked any real leadership and, although he had never been a Scout himself, he felt he should make an effort to fill the gap. This he did, and he did it well, even if there were moments of disaster!

We had a visit last week from the Assistant National Scout Commissioner. We had prepared a big reception for him the week before, but I had got the date wrong! We had been doing 'show' activities for about two hours before we gave him up! As it was he arrived the same day a week later, just after the school had finished, when everyone was in lunch. However they eventually lined up and flagged 'Welcome' in semaphore, but he could not read it because they held their flags crooked! (So he said). He delivered a few well-chosen words about what a Scout *should* be. He said he would ask no questions about my pretensions or qualifications to be helping with a Scout troop because he had an Irish grandmother who held firmly to the maxim that if rules were not made to be broken there would be no need of policemen. He knew full well that they were nil, and was shrewd enough to realise that if I were to follow my natural bent I would invariably hang the Union Jack upside down, though he did not actually say so! He thanked me all the same which was nice of him.

Expeditions

Holidays were the great opportunity. It was at this moment in the year that the essential difference between a volunteer and an ordinary

133

expatriate worker overseas became apparent. As long as he did the job for which he had been requested and remained in the classroom, the volunteer, except for his youth, did not differ from his fellow teachers. But when the school holidays began then his youth came into its own and parties of youngsters, no longer pupils and teacher so much as contemporaries, set off to explore and discover the country in which they were all living. Because he was only short-term the volunteer could afford, paradoxically, to be prodigal with his time. The teacher for whom this was a life work needed to hoard his resources and to recuperate in his holidays in order to run the long steady course before him, but the sprinter, the volunteer, had no such need. This was an experience which would not be repeated for him ever again in quite this same form, and so he gave it all he had and used every facet of the school year to deepen his understanding of the people among whom he worked.

For Sean and Fred in North Borneo, faced with a school situation which was fraught with difficulties, the holidays afforded an opportunity for a different and more informal contact with their pupils. It also gave them the chance to get away from each other. Volunteers stationed in twos faced a very real hazard in their personal association. Thrown much in each other's company, their relationship, like an arranged marriage, could wear very thin, and though we took some trouble to try to match temperaments and talents it was not always possible to do so with complete success. We grew, in fact, to believe that ideally no project should have more than one volunteer, unless it offered a wide variety of work; the difficulties of adjusting to close contact with those of a different race from oneself were as nothing to the difficulties of adjusting to the constant companionship and maybe rivalry, of a strange compatriot.

Not all the expeditions undertaken were a success. Sometimes they were too ambitious, sometimes local conditions defeated the most gallant attempts to defy apathy, or ants, or anti-cyclones. But, whether successful or not, they were nearly always productive of a greater understanding of, and very often of a genuine love for the country and its people.

Each holidays Sean took a small party of his boys into the Borneo interior.

Last holidays I set off into the forest again—this time to place called Pinangah, at the head of the River Kinabatangan an just about in the centre of Borneo. There is a very lively school there which has built most of its buildings itself. The purpose of this journey was twofold. First I wanted to get our boys to rough it a bit, and also get them away from other Chinese and try to get them to realise that they are not the only race in Borneo. The second was to see the school and show them that we were interested in their work and join in with anything they happened to be doing.

The journey was certainly rough enough for the boys. According to the map there was a bridle path all the way but on the fourth day there was only a jungle track, while on the fifth and sixth days there was nothing which I could see, and if we had not had our two carriers with us as guides we would have been quickly lost. Also Lungkat and Limpada, which proudly flaunted themselves on the map as dots, were in fact less than that on the ground. They were non-existent, and how they ever got into the map I don't know. As a result we had to sleep in the forest one night there and one going back. It would have been two but I made everyone go fast and we only took two days through the forest when most people would take three. When I say most I am talking about the three or so people who go every year.

It was a fine place for animals, especially wild pigs. Stately, dowager-looking members of this vast family strolled across the path now and then, or more often scrambled in a very undignified way down banks when caught in their wallows by our approach. The shelters we made for the night were all right until it rained, which it did coming back, and as a good two feet of me poked out at the end I felt it.

The boys were not so good at this, and on the way there anyway were constantly complaining. They were also lazy and I soon found it was a case of doing the work myself or else nagging them. I usually did the first, thinking that example was better than school-mastering, especially on a holiday; but towards the middle of the journey I began to make them do some of it by the simple method of refusing to do it all myself. When it came to the point of not getting any food unless they helped to cook they soon did it. One of them was very good, and in the end all of them had improved and did not even grumble so much.

However as for getting to know and like the Muruts and forgetting the Chinese. The first part they were willing to do – up

135

to a point. They were friendly with our guides and got on well with the boys at Pinangah school. However the second was impossible. I didn't know whether to laugh or cry when we arrived on the first day at our stopping-place for the night, a filthy shack built for travellers and already inhabited by a party of Muruts, when one of the boys turned up his nose and said: 'No. We cannot sleep here. Better we go to Chinese man's house.' I explained to him as gently as I could that we would see no more Chinese until we got to Pinangah. One of the boys forthwith returned home the next day, but the other four stuck it out.

When we got to Pinangah the first thing they did was to go and visit the two Chinese shopkeepers there to take tea. Then they came back gushing about how kind the Chinese were. As one of the shopkeepers was charging us exhorbitant prices, and as the Muruts at the school and the Malay masters were treating us very kindly I suggested that perhaps the Muruts were equally kind. They didn't quite agree about the equally, but since we got back I have heard them saying that the people at the school were very kind.

I and the boys joined in with football. I played with bare feet as my shoes were broken. Then I showed them some gym and got the boys to do some, and then tried to teach the Murut boys a few simple things. The best thing was that the boys saw me working as much as anyone and carrying my own water and washing in the river with everyone else and sleeping with them in their boarding-house. Before this they had only seen government officials who were more aloof.

On the way back, while staying the night at the village of the rowers who had taken us down-river, I did some gym for them as they asked me to, having seen me do it at Pinangah. The women loved it, although I wasn't feeling too happy as a bamboo floor makes a tough landing ground. Having shown photos of self and family, and in the end given most of them away, and also drunk enough rice wine to satisfy them and copied some of their dancing for them and for my own enjoyment, and finally shared two packets of cigarettes with them we were all bosom friends, and I was having a glorious time trying to pick up half of what they were saying to me. By this time they thought I was expert in Malay, and I did not disillusion them. When I really couldn't get what they were saying I just replied 'Ahhhhhh' in a knowing fashion and everyone seemed happy.

This was, for me, the high point of the trip as one old man, who had been very taciturn when I tried to talk to him when he was rowing the boat, now thawed fully and said I was the only 'tuan' he had met whom he liked. From what I could gather he had a rooted dislike for all white men after meeting some curt fellows working for the government, but he said that now he knew that there were some good ones because I had drunk their rice wine and given away all my photos and cigarettes and done some gym for them. In the end I had to go to bed after prolonged thank-you's all round and promises from them that when I came again they would all come and row for me. I could not explain to them that I could not come again as time means nothing to them and they don't understand when I say that I must go back to England before October.

This kind of holiday expedition, repeated in essence in many parts of the world, had an extra complicating factor when it came to Southern Africa. Dick, in Swaziland, by now fully at home in his all-African school, had made a plan with the one other volunteer in the territory, which was both imaginative and courageous.

I have seen quite a bit of Paul, who is five miles away, and we have made plans for the holidays. We are going to take a student each and go camping together round Swaziland. This seems impossible in the Union, unless we want to land up in jail, though perhaps we might risk it in July! I had originally thought that we would hitch-hike around—a European and an African together. I thought, and in fact still do think, that this will prove a problem to the European motorist. I think it worth giving this a try, although the Europeans I have met here say no car will stop. However it will give them something to think about when they see us by the side of the road. They are very quick to give me a lift when I am on my own.

This was the plan, made at a fairly early stage in Dick's year, and he brought it to fruition during the long school holiday. It may not have achieved a great deal where the European motorists were concerned, as most of them simply thought of the black man of the party as a servant, but it did cement for Dick and Joseph, who was his companion, a firm friendship.

With exams behind me I went off with Paul and one of my

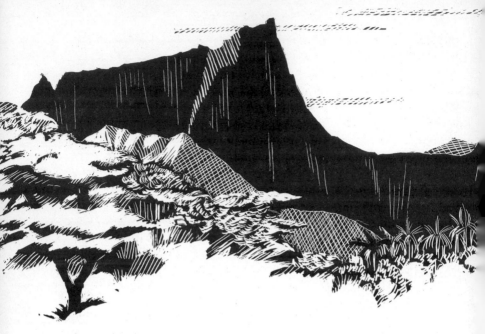

MOUNT KINABALU, NORTH BORNEO

students, Joseph—whom incidentally I am sure will go a long way and be one of the leading lights in Swaziland in twenty years' time—to see as much of the country as we could in a short space of time, as Joseph had to go and work in order to get enough money to pay his fees at Basutoland University, where he goes in February.

We only had a small tent which could just manage three and it also seemed likely that the weather would be terrible as it was the rainy season. However this did not happen and the scheme turned out to be a magnificent success. We hitch-hiked our way round—often in the backs of open trucks and covered most of the country totalling three hundred and fifty miles. We found some splendid camping spots.

We stayed one night near to Joseph's brother's kraal—he is a chief—and exchanged gifts. The chief provided us with a chicken and in return we gave him a few cigarettes! Everywhere we went people were very inquisitive—not surprising as this sort of thing is unheard of here—although as a matter of fact the Swazis are a very inquisitive people. They were all impressed when told, and even the Europeans stopped regularly to give us a lift, merely remarking about Joseph, 'Is this your boy?' or 'Is this chap with you?'

Not all trips were as simple to operate as this one; occasionally they involved quite complicated administration and planning and as, in fact, no plan ever went without hitches in the under-developed countries, what seemed at first sight a fairly straightforward journey could end up very differently.

In Western Nigeria William had made quite elaborate plans to take a party of boys from his school over to Eastern Nigeria, partly as an educational visit, partly to a social service project helping to clear the site of a new grammar school. This involved a journey of some hundreds of miles and a crossing of the River Niger on one of the major ferries of Nigeria. Journeys of this sort were invariably made by three- or five-ton lorry along bumpy, dusty roads edged with forest, or palm trees, or, in the East, wide vistas of rolling scrub land.

We went in the St Michael's lorry, packed tighter than sardines, and if our lorry had virtues, space and springs and reliability were not among them. We started off cheerfully enough, singing hymns with great gusto and impeccable harmony, until after six miles we had a puncture. As the spare tyre was also punctured we had to empty out and trek back to Emevor; while the lorry dashed off at high speed back to Ughelli to repair itself.

Soon after one o'clock it returned and we set off again (not before one boy — the senior prefect I regret to say — had decided that he was not quite so anxious to go after all, but, having been told that there was no question of his money being returned, reluctantly relented) only this time to get rather less far before we had another puncture. These minor mishaps effectively dampened most of the enthusiasm of the party, particularily the grammar school boys, who had suffered in the past from the failure of this same lorry and were not anxious to repeat the experience.

This time the same senior prefect and another boy firmly took out their cases and announced that they were going to trek home rather than set foot in that lorry again. Eventually I persuaded them to get back in again, but by the time the puncture was mended the atmosphere was pretty grim, and I spent the next thirty miles with my heart in my mouth in case we should get another puncture, when I think they really would have gone on strike, and our 'adventure' would have come to an abrupt and ignominious conclusion . . .

Our destination was a town (in the Eastern Region) which is the home of my Ibo house-companion who organised the expedition. As soon as we got there our lorry left us to be repaired and we were involved in a good deal of expense charting transport to take us to interesting places . . .

The lorry, having had extensive repairs, continued to fail us at every possible turn causing irritation which in turn led to our sometimes having to pull the donkey towards the carrot, when the donkey preferred the haystack behind. But the party mixed well, and the irritation was on the surface only and it disappeared as soon as its cause disappeared. One evening some of us went to a public debate at the British Council on the motion 'The Intellectual: a Curse to Society', during the course of which I, being almost the only European there, and feeling sufficiently protected by a white skin, was impertinent enough to accuse the formidable African intellectual who was proposing the motion of twisted reasoning. Before a lively adult audience who were loud in their agreement of anything one said, or disagreement as the case might be, one almost captured some of the thrill of the demagogue! I did not come back with the party but went to Benin for a couple of nights, where I stayed with one of the grammar school boys, whose father keeps a store there, before returning home. For a couple of days in what remained of the holidays I went on a bicycle tour of part of the Isoko district, with another boy from the grammer school. We went to a town on the River Niger, three of us on two bicycles (one of which had a puncture) taking it in turns to carry each other and be carried on the bar, and we passed through several towns on the way where I saw some of the schoolboys in their homes. A hot and mosquito-ridden night, during which I shared a bed with my escort, was partly compensated for by two dips in the river, which is somewhat public but was very refreshing. I greatly enjoyed this short tour, which made me realise more fully the primitiveness of the background from which the boys mostly come – something of which although one is aware, when one only sees them in school seems very remote – not that they live in luxury at school (or in squalor at home for that matter).

This account of a school journey may not seem very startling or revolutionary, yet, in his quiet way, William was a pioneer. It would certainly be the first time that his schoolboys had ridden turn and turn about with a British boy on the bar of the bicycle and put him up in the spare room behind their father's store.

When William left the school clubbed together to give him a parting gift. They presented him with a full set of Western Nigerian robes, and William, touched by their obvious appreciation and affection, promised that he would wear them on the day that Nigeria gained her Independence which came a few weeks after he had arrived back at home in England. When the First of October arrived William was up at University and the difficulty of fulfilling his promise to his pupils in Nigeria was suddenly presented to him with embarrassing clearness. How was he to appear in full Yoruba costume without cutting a ridiculous and pretentious figure? It never occurred to him that the simplest way would be to forget that he had made any such promise. In the end he solved the problem in a way that was very characteristic. He rose very early indeed, dressed himself carefully in the splendid and flamboyant garments of West Africa, went out and got on his bicycle and then cycled furiously, yards of material billowing out behind him, through the early, empty streets of Cambridge. Nigeria would never know it, but her Independence was sincerely celebrated in many ways which she would have considered very strange.

WEST AFRICAN MARKET MAMMY

CHAPTER IV

Problems and Perplexities

TERRY

EVEN though, at the last moment, he might have qualms about his own inadequacy, the prospect of a year overseas was for every volunteer a glamorous and adventurous one. He knew that there would be hardships, but he geared himself to meet them and prepared to live simply and rough.

We, for our part, were well aware that his real difficulties would not be those of physical deprivation but would be the problems of human relationships and personal growth inherent in undertaking an adult job in the ordinary world — whether in Birmingham or Borneo. We tried to forwarn each volunteer of the dilemmas with which he might be confronted, and to assure him of confidence in his ability to meet them; we promised him all the help and advice that could be given at long distance; but, ultimately, each one had to meet his problems on his own and deal with them as best he could in the light of common sense and the local situation.

The moment he stepped off the ship or train or aeroplane into the country where he was to work the volunteer was brought face to face with the one big change in his life which was to affect all he did, a change which, in a sense, it had been impossible for him to visualise accurately beforehand: he was suddenly and simply an adult, no longer shielded from problems and difficulties but expected to shoulder his full share of responsibility. This was what he had longed for. Over a period of months, or even of years, each volunteer had being thinking of himself as a young man, and trying to impress upon everyone else that he really was such. Now, when those around him took this fact for granted, he suddenly realised that to himself he was still a boy. This recognition, the result of immersion in a common human world, was valuable in the effect that it had on the volunteer's whole approach to his work. It gave him humility, and it quickly disabused him of any notion that he came as anything but a rather lowly helper.

The problems that arose fell into several catagories but they were almost never concerned with physical discomforts. Most volunteers expected to live with a minimum of civilised gadgetry in a mud hut: the disillusion came when they found themselves, as sometimes happened, in air-conditioned modernity. But their own living conditions interested them very little and were rarely the subject of complaint or upset. Similarly health figured hardly at all in the letters home. This was not because every volunteer survived his year without illness, quite a large number suffered from stomach trouble or malaria at one time or another, and prickly heat or sensitiveness to insect bites were also fairly common. One or two volunteers had more serious ailments, but on the whole their health was not a cause of anxiety, either to us or to them. For them illness in any form was simply an interruption in the job and as such not to be dwelt on unduly.

Graham wrote from Sarawak:

> I sweat; I itch; I have skin fungus; I am hot. I do not sleep; I am very tired; I teach all day long; I work in the mornings and evenings; I write; I learn Dayak; I find life *very tough*. After a month hard at it these are my first impressions, reactions and feelings.
>
> It is certainly teaching me to have great control in that I have no one to turn to and moan to. As I write this I am perspiring more than freely. Bathing is no longer a pleasure as it means drying oneself afterwards and that usually starts all the patches of fungus (almost everywhere) itching and irritating again. I have been told to put Calamine Powder on, but this only seems to add to the general discomfiture — I wouldn't mind so much if it didn't mean sleepless nights — it looks as though I am having a good moan after all! I just grin and bear it — it seems to me to be the best policy.

The other sex was not a problem either. Again there were a few exceptions but on the whole the age of the volunteers stood them in good stead here. Unlike graduates they felt that there was plenty of time for girls in the future and the attraction of an adult job for the first time heavily outweighed any desire to relax in feminine company. They were too busy and too involved in the excitement and challenge of their jobs to have any time for philandering.

We took considerable trouble to try to fit volunteers into the kind of religious – or indeed non-religious – background that accorded with their own spirits. Nevertheless this did not prevent occasions arising when the volunteer suffered a deep sense of shock on meeting active Christianity, or active atheism, overseas. Neither resembled the passive, tolerant, accepted varieties that he was accustomed to at home. He could be repelled or attracted by what he found, but he was, almost always, compelled to reassess his own religious views and to think a good deal more positively and deeply about the issues than he had done before. It was a girl who wrote:

> I think to say you are a Christian means something very different here from saying the same in England... strangely enough it's with the English people that I feel most necessity to choose my words, but with the local people it isn't necessary because with many races living together they accept ideas and are only too eager to discuss the subjects usually avoided in England when not among people you know ... I think the reason why I've always resisted becoming a Christian is because at school we were made to go to church and to be honest I was generally bored, except when the sermon was interesting. Yet here we have prayers in the evening and these are so different. They are so very simple and sincere, praying for the people around in their daily work.

Her ability to write about spiritual problems was, however, exceptional, and little of the thinking that preoccupied the volunteers on this subject went down on paper. Often it was only indirectly, and much later, that we discovered how radically this experience had affected the lives of some of our volunteers.

As might be expected a major difficulty lay in the volunteer's relationships to other people, particularily the complex and delicate web which was the association of himself with his own fellow-countrymen and the nationals of the country in which they both worked. We had anticipated that a constant cause of friction in most countries might lie in a difference of outlook between the volunteer and his own compatriots of á generation or so older. The volunteer arrived untrammelled by a traditional attitude to countries overseas, and owing allegiance to a set of ideas rather than to a Service. He started out to make his friends and find his leisure occupations among the local people rather than among his own countrymen. This was obviously a situation full of possibilities of misunderstanding. The volunteers were most carefully briefed that they were forming a bridge rather than taking sides, and that their job was as much to convince their own countrymen that fresh attitudes were both possible and desirable as to show increasingly nationalistic indigenous young people that sympathetic involvement in their affairs was not incompatible with friendly discussion and criticism.

James was one of the few volunteers who had done his National Service in the Far East. This made him older, in years and in experience than most of the others, but he also was waiting to go up to university. James was articulate and intelligent, and as this was not his first spell overseas he had some background on which to base his conclusions. He went to Northern Rhodesia as an Assistant District Officer.

I last wrote from out in the district, from a place I was very sorry to leave three weeks ago. However the Provincial Commissioner thought it a good idea for me to see something of urban Northern Rhodesia before I leave and arranged for my transfer to Lusaka. And while being sorry to leave a place and a people which harbours many happy memories, I am glad at the same time to have an opportunity of seeing something of town life and administration — it is, as I thought in my last letter, very different.

Perhaps the most notable difference is that almost any form of social contact with Africans here is taboo among the vast majority of Europeans, in a way that it was not at Serenje. That is not to say that it was common practice there — but at least one was not branded as a crank or even upstart, as one can easily be here. Though, if I may put it this way, I took pains while at Serenje not to alienate biased opinion for this very reason — to be dismissed as an eccentric in ones 'persistence in fraternising' with the African does not help to bring the races of this Territory together — if anything it accentuates the problem and the African himself tends to confuse one with a missionary, which is something I don't pretend to be.

Here in Lusaka, I am living in a Government Hostel for

145

European Civil Servants – a soulless place of impersonal comforts when I compare it with my small house at Serenje, and one where a major disturbance would be provoked, I fancy, were I to introduce an African into its precincts. Nor is it entirely easy for me to visit Africans on their own ground though there is nothing statutory against it. I was warned, by African friends, before leaving Serenje, not to go into the Lusaka township suburbs after dark lest I fall prey to marauding thugs – and this applied equally to the black as to the white man, except that the white man is obviously a preferable victim. And though I've not been the subject of any violent demonstration, having been hostilely taunted while leaving one such suburb after visiting a friend late one afternoon, I caught a glimpse of what it must be like to be constantly on the receiving end of the less violent but equally wounding attitude indulged in by the majority of Europeans towards Africans – one which imputes unspeakable despicability. One thing is certain, the 'troublesome' African of today is such by virtue of the advent of the white man. Had he not come then Africa would even now be only one hundred years this side of the iron age instead of two thousand – and it is at the door of the white innovators that blame must be laid if things go wrong. One begins to realise that the problem child of Northern Rhodesia is not the backward African but the artisan class of European.

Something which has struck me very forcibly is the burning desire of almost every African I know to go to the U.K. This ambition sometimes smacks of Dick Whittington but in general it is held in the valid belief that in England they will enjoy an Englishman's rights – something they can't enjoy here – yet. May I give you a very basic example of discrimination which causes me to doubt even Government's avowed intention to smooth out racial prejudice? The Lusaka Boma is a brand new building completed only a few months ago. In it work a dozen District and Departmental Officers and several Africans of officer status – some of whom have been in the U.K. – and a score of African clerks. However in this futuristic building at opposite ends of passages on two floors are identical toilet arrangements but with the distinction that one set bears a label 'Gentlemen' and one 'African Men'. I venture to say that this sort of thing more than niggles an African who is doing his best to live after the European way, and it astounds me.

I shall be truly sorry to leave Northern Rhodesia in a month's time. It has been the most eye-opening experience of my life as well as being a profound exercise in self-knowledge.

It was, perhaps obviously, in Africa that racial problems were most overt. Here, where the colour difference was greatest, discrimination was at its most open. It could be argued that this was even an advantage, forcing recognition of race prejudice as a problem and forbidding easy complacency. In countries in which, ostensibly, a multiracial community worked the volunteer found himself in a much more delicate and confusing situation.

British Guiana, in 1959, had two volunteers. On the whole the countries of the Western Hemisphere, whatever the predominant colour of their majorities, confronted the rest of the world with a claim to be united as peoples. On the surface it often appeared that this was indeed so, and that the cradle of the true multiracial state must lie in this part of the world. Underneath, however, lay deep cleavages, which could well hold the seeds of greater disaster, just because they were hidden and rarely consciously acknowledged.

In British Guiana Colin, working in the interior at Orealla was outside the confusing currents of racial antagonism. For him the relationship with the Amerindians was still the simple and uncomplicated one of the very early days of British overseas expansion, even although he himself approached the work in a fraternal rather than paternal spirit. But for David, teaching in the Bauxite town of Mackenzie, the situation was very different.

Mackenzie was an industrial town with a large Canadian population. David went to help as a teacher at the secondary school which, thanks to Canadian assistance, was very well equipped. The school was multiracial, taking pupils from every local community, Canadian, Guianese, Indian. The atmosphere was a sophisticated one, and at first David found this hard to bear, envying Colin his simpler and more primitive project. However he was an extremely intelligent boy who recognised the essence of the challenge in working among an educated elite.

The local people hold Europeans in such high esteem that anything I say or do becomes a topic of conversation. I must always be setting an example to them. I regard the most important section of my work to be in meeting people. This is not difficult because the Guianese are naturally hospitable. I am glad that the

147

local people are quite frank in discussing problems of racial prejudice, etc. What is more they bring up the subject themselves!...
Unlike the headmaster of the school, I have already been accepted to some extent into the life of the coloured community. This was due to the fact that at no time was I living with the Canadian staff: an invaluable asset! The line of demarcation is very strong unfortunately!

David, who was a good musician, joined the all-coloured dance band at the staff club, and he was accepted with great friendliness. He was given the feeling that he came between the Canadians and the Guianese, acceptable to both and possibly in a position to form a bridge between them. Had he been more experienced he might have recognised that this central situation could also mean that he was the pivot in a tug-of-war. Unfortunately he was in for a rude shock.

I wrote to you about the relationship between myself and the Guianese staff of the school. I'm afraid events since have proved me completely wrong in my judgement. In fact I have realised with a shock that there is a great deal of hostility under the surface — partly because they think I'm taking the job away from a Guianese teacher. Also because they are looking for any opportunity to show that I am privileged because of my colour. Naturally this has depressed me a good deal, because it is hard to act normally under these conditions. The continual curb on one's tongue is a terrible strain for someone as quick tempered as me! Anyway I'm living with it and things work out.

In this case the prejudice worked in the opposite direction and David was really the victim of it. This was not an easy year, and much of it David endured rather than enjoyed. But he made a success of it and at the end he could write and say:

I am quite certain — despite minor setbacks which one must always encounter — that I would not have missed this year for anything. The staff of the school and I have made a friendly compromise. The great shock is to realise that the year is so nearly over.

Discrimination can take many, and sometimes subtle, forms. In Guiana and in Rhodesia there were feelings of inferiority and superiority involved, but in North Borneo it was a clash of equals.

Fred, who in any case lacked self-confidence, found his Chinese pupils very difficult.

As you probably well know the Chinese are as proud and independent as the British themselves, and certainly regard their culture as superior to any others. I can't blame them. However herein lies the difficulty. I am teaching the top two forms of the school, and they are all approximately the same age as myself, and many are older. They seem to have the same objection to being taught and disciplined by one as old as them or younger as kids back in England have. Consequently I am temporarily riding quite a black storm and making a number of enemies. I don't mind this, but the trouble is that it is affecting me in my other activities, and I am rather like a run-down clockwork machine. I am now in the process of winding myself up again, and I pray that I can do it. I have been feeling very sorry for myself, which is fatal, but difficult not to do. Somehow I've got to plough on regardless.

Sean, too, although more sure of himself, found the atmosphere of antagonism that greeted them at first difficult to cope with.

Although I have made good friends among the boys and many of them come into our house for a talk now and then, there is still a lot of antagonism — that is perhaps too strong — anyway a feeling of wariness all round. I feel it in one of my classes and it makes teaching very difficult in the class... it makes me nervous and then I don't teach very well.

In the nature of things it was difficult for a volunteer to take a long-term view. His own time was limited and his youth inclined him to expect immediate solutions. Fred never really got over his feeling of having been a failure, and both he and Sean had grave doubts about their value to the school. But those who watched from the outside had no doubt and their successor, when he arrived, did not have to face nearly so much hostility.

It was surprising how sometimes a firm stand by a volunteer could crumble barriers which had appeared impenetrable. It could be that local opinion had become frozen into certain attitudes in which it no longer wholly believed but lacked the ability to break a fixed pattern. Then a volunteer, coming in from outside, uncommitted and belonging to no local line-up, could step forward and find to his surprise that others quietly closed up behind him. In Southern

THAI STUDENT

Rhodesia, Robert was responsible for several of these unspectacular small waves of progress.

Jonathan and I took a party of teachers into a political brains trust, and not only did it serve as a good influence in amongst the large European audience, but it also strengthened our ties with the teachers.

Louis Armstrong came to Salisbury to give a couple of shows, with reduced prices for schoolchildren; so, after holding a talent competition in the school, I took our forty best entertainers along. We were in the same seats as the Salisbury non-African schools, but half-way through they were allowed to go through the enclosure to get a close-up view. This was naturally unfair, but as it was under the auspices of the American Information Services a short complaint to the management soon put things right, and the several hundred African schoolchildren there were allowed to move right into the arena.

A major triumph this week, to my mind anyway, as it has been an ambition ever since I arrived, is that the Senior Young Farmer's Club is now multiracial. Ever since I took the three boys with me on the week-end course at Inyanga, I've noticed that there are several members in the club with liberal views. So, at the annual general meeting, having been elected vice-chairman and undertaken the job of press secretary, I put forward a resolution that the club's policy be changed. The opposition amounted to three, so it was successfully carried. The only thing now is to see that it comes into effect.

The most critical eye was cast on their own compatriots. Here the volunteers felt entitled to express an opinion and it was, on the whole, a balanced one. They did not hesitate to give their admiration where they felt it to be deserved, but equally they condemned where condemnation was due. It was interesting to find that they shared with the countries in which they worked a revolt against the paternalistic attitude which so many of the older Britons had inevitably grown up with, and this, unconsciously perhaps, drew them closer to their indigenous contemporaries. Both coveted independence. It was a reflection of a universal redirection of social thinking, which made these volunteers in some ways more attuned to the world in which they found themselves than older men who had lived in it all their lives.

In the Gambia, in a teacher training centre which happened to be housed in what had originally been the buildings used by the big Gambia egg-producing scheme—which had turned out a disastrous failure—Roderic and Neil found themselves receiving a good deal of unwanted pity. Had they needed to be reconciled to their surroundings, which in fact they did not, this was the way to do it.

> People tend to think of us as poor ill-cared-for children and the thought of being 'forced to live cheek by jowl with the students in an old hen house' sets the European population saying all sorts of things against the college Principal.

In fact the 'old hen house' was a reasonable stone-built building, more than adequate by the standards of the country; the real reason for the commiseration was that they lived in such close proximity to the students, who were of course all African.

Exactly the same sort of feeling was displayed several thousand miles away on the other side of Africa in Bechuanaland, where Mike, going to teach in an all-African school, wrote:

> The attitude of the Europeans here is an interesting one. My own feelings at coming here were great feelings of excitement but my first brush with the Europeans soon dashed these. I arrived at M. on a Thursday and on a Saturday I was taken to the capital to introduce me. I found myself at a cocktail party surrounded by almost the entire European community. When they knew I was to spend a year at M. I heard such comments as: 'Well, you must get out as often as you can—all these black people,' or 'After a year you'll deserve a medal,' 'After all they're not like us.' 'Poor—.' On the drive back I was perhaps more apprehensive but such is the friendliness and courtesy that one could not fail to be blissfully happy and at home.

For a single volunteer, unsupported by group solidarity, this could have been a traumatic experience. Feeling himself out of step he might have reacted violently towards an extreme. In fact none did, and I think this was due to very careful briefing before they left about the kind of situation which might arise, and their recognition of their own position in a whole fresh approach to working overseas, which gave them stability while demanding responsibility. This did not preclude a certain groping for identity, especially among those who came from sheltered backgrounds. It was, in fact, a girl who put something of this into words.

One of the most difficult things I have found in my contacts with people here is that I don't know if the incidents I see and the way people behave is peculiar to Penang, the East or the world in general. Being at boarding-school for seven years meant that really I don't know what life is like in an English community. During the holidays I was always going away and I've never been at home without the feeling of being 'on holiday'. How I wish I could go back to England to have a look round and then come back here again to see if my impressions are changed.

Perhaps this acknowledgement of inexperience, which was shared by most volunteers, was one of their assets, making them both sensitive and curious towards the world around them, and keeping them always prepared to learn from their hosts as well as to give.

. . . . .

Alastair went from Scotland to Thailand, to teach in a secondary school. This was an important request, one of the first from a fully independent country outside the Commonwealth, and they asked for five volunteers, three to teach English and two apprentices to act as instructors at a Graduate Engineering College. We chose these five very carefully; we were very pleased that the Government of Thailand was asking us for volunteers and aware that this might have far-reaching consequences for the future. The Thai request had taken eighteen months to come to fruition. Months of careful negotiation and two fortunate visits by my husband to Bangkok were required, not because the Thais were unwilling, they were not, but because the nature of bureaucracy in Thailand was complicated, tortuous and slow.

Something of this complexity on a lesser level the volunteers were also going to have to face, and, inevitably, there would be frustration. At the same time they were going to work with a people of high artistic sensibility, courteous, sensitive, kindly, and who never in their long history had been anything but independent. We required to send volunteers who were themselves sensitive, sensible and intelligent. Alastair was all these things; he was also extremely handsome.

He travelled by courtesy of the Royal Air Force to Singapore, and from there took a train up the long Malayan Peninsula and into Thailand. In itself this journey was an adventure, involving a night in a crowded carriage where he made his first acquaintance with some young Thais going back to their own country. When the train reached the border and customs officials boarded it, Alastair was astonished and touched to be vouched for by his fellow travellers, 'He is our friend. He is going to teach our people.'

An hour out of Bangkok he managed to get himself along the crowded corridor and into the tiny lavatory. Here he changed into clean clothes and made himself as fresh and respectable as the circumstances permitted. It was time well spent. When the train drew into the platform he found a small deputation to meet him, from the Thai Ministry of Education and from the British Council, and a garland of flowers was hung around his neck. With some hesitation and embarrassment he joined his hands together in the Thai gesture of greeting and bowed his head over them.

Alastair went into a very good secondary school set in beautiful surroundings just outside Bangkok. At first he found this difficult to accept having imagined himself dealing with the challenge of wild and primitive places. However he had agreed to go where he was sent and he set himself to become involved with the people among whom he found himself. They were charming and he was soon friends with many and at home with all, and on very good terms with his headmaster whom he admired. The difficulties, and there were difficulties, were not in this instance problems of personal relations, they were rather the clash of two totally different ways of looking at life. Alastair, whose own school brought its boys up in a tradition of energetic leadership, found here that his pupils reacted to certain situations in a manner that was the very opposite of his own and his very sensitivity, which made him the right volunteer for this country, also involved him in a real personal dilemma.

The main trouble is that Thais, kind and peace-loving as they may be, are not prepared to make a decision or take responsibility for anything. Their idea of paradise is to lie on one's bed, looking at the sky and doing nothing, while the rest of the world moves on. In some ways I do not totally disagree with this attitude, but in the atmosphere which it creates it is extremely difficult to start anything new or to make any change.

During the examinations there was widespread cheating all round, with, believe it or not, conversations. The Thai teachers knew that it was going on but somehow they did not make any attempt to stop it, either because they did not wish to face the reality that they were cheating, or else they were frightened of the students.

What could the volunteer do when he is confronted with the piercing fact that his friends cheat and have little knowledge of the seriousness of their act? Either he turns a blind eye and everyone is happy, but if he does this he abandons all the principles for which he stands and only cheats himself, or he decides to attempt to stop it knowing that he might break some friendships in doing so. Well, when I saw that the teachers were not going to take any action to stop it, even though I hinted at it a little, I decided to steer my own course. I knew that it would be no good just to go up to them and say 'stop cheating', because they would just lose face, so instead I set about it as their friend. If I saw them passing on information to a friend (they believe that they must help one another in true Thai fashion) my face would become very heavy and sad, and they would stop. Then in the evening if he was in my room I would pretend to be very depressed and without fail he would ask me why. When I gave him the reason he would become very emotional, eyelids flicking up and down and looking as if he was about to burst into tears at any moment, because he was so grieved that he should have been the cause of my unhappiness. Rather pathetic, but you know it worked and within a few days they knew that I hated it and it made me unhappy, and it practically stopped except for a few isolated instances.

The other day a boy came up to me and said, 'Thank you for helping me to be good,' and this brings out the point that the Thai boy inwardly wishes to behave well, but has not got the will-power to turn temptations aside.

One can smile, in these days of sophisticated cynicism, at the simplicity of this approach, but could there be a more intuitively

sympathetic handling of a problem which involved differing East-West values? And one of the major strengths of the young volunteer is amply illustrated here, they were not afraid of goodness in the way in which an adult is.

If in Thailand it was unfamiliar values which were difficult to handle, in Nyasaland, hardly surprisingly, it was politics which proved to be the stumbling-block.

Jonathan was also in a very good secondary school, indeed the best equipped in Nyasaland. For most of the time he got on well with his pupils and liked them as they liked him, but one of the disconcerting aspects of working in a country with an explosive political situation was the way in which, overnight, friends could be changed into enemies. It was also particularily difficult for a boy from a British school, where politics rarely entered into the atmosphere in a vital manner, to adjust himself to a school in Nyasaland where politics were the stuff of daily living, and the schoolboys often in the forefront of political campaigning. Temperamentally Jonathan was not very suited to this uncertain climate. He was quiet and conscientious and it worried him deeply that the boys, whom he grew to like very much, could apparently dispense with his friendship at a moment's notice because of what he felt to be a false mass emotion.

Jonathan was in Nyasaland at a very difficult time politically. The whole position of the country within what was then the Central African Federation was in question, and a commission had been set up to consider it. The members of this commission were at this time in Nyasaland taking information from different groups and individuals, and this in itself was a delicate matter. Dr Banda, then a powerful anti-Federation political leader was in prison, and this, as so often in colonial territories, had increased his local prestige rather than diminished it.

The school in which Jonathan worked took the elite from all over the country. It was the premier government secondary school and many of its boys would go on to positions of importance in government and civil service. They were also considerably closer to the height of their ambitions than their equivalent in Britain might be because Nyasaland had so few young men with any sort of higher education. In the circumstances it was hardly surprising that they were already vociferous in their country's political struggles, and it may be that the situation was not made easier for Jonathan by the fact that a number of the staff were European, exerting a pull which made his precarious central position a matter of considerable nervous tension.

The political situation does not help matters, and the general staff-pupil relationship at the present is not very good, but I take the line that politics are rather outside my 'terms of reference'. I hope I am not falling into the category of people who are not willing to get up and argue for the right. If I keep off the subject among the boys, this is hardly so in the staff room where constant (friendly) verbal battles are waged.

Later:

Things have grown no easier on the political front out here. I think it is true to say that tension in the school mounted, especially while the Monckton Commission was here, and that we were very fortunate to pass through that particular phase without any real trouble. I must say that at that time I almost despaired. Staff-pupil relationship was frankly bad and I was treated as a member of staff, even by the senior boys whom I did not teach and to whom I had tried to give a completely different impression. Worst of all the boys here seemed to distrust Europeans in general, however friendly and sincere they were. I am glad to say that phase is largely over. Strangely enough the release of Dr Banda seems to have done the trick. There is a much improved spirit in the school, and as far as I am concerned the boys have shown a far greater tendency to accept my friendship. I admit I am hoping for great things next term, though it is rather disconcerting to feel that one's success or failure with the boys (though that is perhaps going too far) depends on the political situation.

Later:

Things I am bound to admit are not going too well here at the moment. Wednesday, unfortunately, brought the upset. Once again it was politics, my Number One enemy. Dr Banda held a rally in the town and naturally all the boys wanted to go. Unfortunately it was in school hours, so that they all (with the exception of the sixth form, who were taken by the headmaster) were forbidden to go, and, as we were expecting trouble the headmaster especially went round warning them of the consequences of disobedience. Well, immediately after break they simply walked out on us, just like that. We found only four of two hundred who stayed behind, and they had done so more out of accident than design. I'm bound to say that the general opinion was to suspend the school until next term, but the ruling came from higher up that about twenty should be suspended and the rest should submit an apology and should receive no teaching for a week. The tragedy, as far as I am concerned, is that the happy relations between staff and pupils which had become much more evident, particularily after Dr Banda's release, have vanished in one morning.

Douglas, who followed Jonathan in the same school, had a different, and perhaps more suitable, temperament. Cheerful, detached, faintly ironic, he also found a political situation which was somewhat eased by the slow movement in Nyasaland towards inevitable independence from the Federation. It is interesting and entertaining to read his assessment of the boys.

One week-end I and six boys spent the afternoon climbing the local mountain and we had a long chat at the top. I must say they are extraordinarily interesting to talk to; I have compiled a list of their characteristics as follows:
Tendency to talk politics;
Interest in co-education;
Interest in all things musical;
Love of dancing;
Slowness of movement, physical and sometimes mental;
Interest in English schools, with special reference to bullying(!!);
Tendency to prefer work to games, owing to tremendous value attached to passing exams.
They are also extremely bitter against the government, because it makes them pay £10 per annum school fees, are quite sure it takes fifteen years to learn the piano, are equally sure that Nyasaland, with twenty-three native graduates, could govern herself now, and have a marked tendency to play tin whistles, made in Birmingham at all hours of the day.

.   .   .   .   .

The problem of lack of co-operation in its many facets — which could include apathy, idleness, misunderstanding, the difference in the concept of time between tropical and temperate countries — was a recurring one everywhere. The volunteers tried all sorts of solutions, and learned many hard lessons themselves in doing so. There was no golden rule, no panacea that could be put in an airmail envelope and flown out to them; they had to solve their own problems by trial and error and patient concentration. Sometimes they succeeded; sometimes they failed.

Perhaps this, which was an undramatic sort of difficulty, was one of the hardest to cope with, and volunteers often felt that it pinpointed some inadequacy in themselves as well as in other people and became, in consequence, depressed.

In North Borneo:

When you have prepared a lesson rather well and made your points clearly (so you think) it is depressing to look out on a sea of stony faces who seem to be unwilling even to try and learn from you.

Sean amplified this and gave some indication of how he and Fred had tackled the situation.

We had two things to fight against. First, lack of response; second, language. The first was by far the worst. It is now, thank goodness, over. The first week, though, we talked to an audience whose faces didn't flicker. We didn't know whether they understood or not. They refused to raise their hands when we asked them, 'Anyone who doesn't understand raise your hand.' Yet two or three questions show that usually 75% did not understand. Apparently there were two reasons for this; one, fear of losing face, two, fear of being asked a lot of questions in English. So we were faced with a problem; we didn't know whether we were over-explaining or under-explaining, and the blankness and

TEACHER

159

'oriental' impassiveness of their faces was getting us down. In the end we began to long for a good honest riot just to show they were alive!

The problem is now solved, partly by the fact that they are no longer so shy with us and partly because we waged a week-long battle against it. My campaign was divided into two. Firstly to try to combat this 'face' idea. I gave them two long talks on how brave I thought it was to put up their hands if everyone was frightened to and how cowardly the others were. Secondly, to allay their fears about hard additional questions for those who put up their hands. I told them that if they did I would not ask them difficult questions but answer theirs. The clinching blow came when six people put up their hands to say they knew a word and I said, 'Right, all the others know this word, do they?' 'Yes, sir', 'O.K. Everyone except those six will now write out a sentence using the word!' In the words of Bernard Miles, 'That 'ad 'em!'

In outside activities, too, this same problem appeared. Sean used similar tactics in an attempt to resolve it, but here, as in a great many other places all over the world and in Britain too, non-co-operation was a facet of the universal human quandary of getting people to work together for a common purpose — a feature of which was that it seemed equally difficult whether they disliked, were indifferent to, or greatly desired the ultimate object.

The English-speaking club now meets every week and has a very good attendance. I have got some of the boys doing jobs, for instance a secretary making minutes and reading them at the beginning of each meeting and a chairman looking after attendance and any general matters I want taken care of. The meetings are a success and they enjoy them. I make them varied with singing, word games and crosswords, debates, talks by the boys and even one of these short debate games which I call 'sharp practices'. All these are good for them to overcome their shyness of speaking English, and also to improve their English as well as giving them some fun and taking their minds off work. However again it is all me.

In Somaliland Peter and David found themselves dealing with a national temperment which they were hard put to it to understand. At this time Somaliland was just about to gain Independence, and incidentally to leave the Commonwealth in doing so in order to join with that part of the country which had been Italian Somalia. There was no real struggle about this Independence and little anti-British feeling, but among the fiercely proud Somalis political parties had sprung up, themselves reflecting all the national strengths and weaknesses in the bitterness of their partisanship.

Party politics penetrated into the school to an extent that even Jonathan in Nyasaland had not experienced, and the result was that such matters as the elections of sports committees were bedevilled by feuds of extreme virulence resulting in strikes and boycotts which disrupted the whole of school life. David had written: 'We find it difficult to conceive of anyone taking such things so to heart that they even allow it to interfere with the friendships they make, and decisions they take; this is not friendly rivalry but bitter hatred.' These political divisions were combined with a volatile and extreme approach to living, and a strong feeling among schoolboys that any sort of manual labour was degrading to an educated man, all of which added up to a situation which was totally alien, temperamentally and in every other way, to Peter and David, themselves quiet, persistent, law-abiding and humble, from respectable unrebellious backgrounds. In the circumstances it was perhaps surprising that both sides came to admire and respect each other, and to form real and continuing friendships; but a closer look would reveal that it was the very antithesis of their qualities which enabled this to happen. Had Peter and David been themselves quick-tempered and 'angry' the relationship which they did manage to build up would have been impossible, and much of their work would never have been accomplished.

We had arranged our Sports Day on the Thursday. It was a fair success but, as well as other sports, was boycotted by one of the political parties (representing about a third of the school) and also removing some of the best competitors. As with everything the Somalis are completely disinterested in such things until they start and then they are full of enthusiasm; so that when the heats started much interest was shown and we felt we had not wasted our time with our persistence.

Prior to the sports we spent a full week preparing and marking out jumping-pits, running-tracks, hockey and football pitches. Some inconsiderate person put a ditch between the two sports pitches necessitating the building of bridges for the running-track,

161

but this was simpler than we dared to hope, especially with the use of piping from the Public Works Department. We marked out a four-lane, four-lap running-track plus 100 yards sprint lanes, but unfortunately we were unable to obtain any volunteers to do work that was considered to be coolie work (and one pupil openly confessed that he believed England had a despicable class distinction). We asked for volunteers to dig out the two jumping-pits — none — next day I asked the Scouts to help fetch a lorryload of sand — a welcome response, but after we had fetched sand (forty minutes riding, ten minutes digging) they were exhausted and wouldn't help to dig the pits further, and several complained because I would not go home and make tea for them which they had missed. The following afternoon we were left to fetch three tons of sand alone, and even the driver just stood back and watched us — such is class distinction! However I paint a very black picture, please do not think we hold any of this against the Somalis, we find it hard to understand but have come to accept it as it is evidently the natural Somali way and hence there is little we can do to alter it.

In one way this problem of apathy was, in itself, the justification for Voluntary Service Overseas. It was not only those from other countries who were concerned by the attitude of mind of the educated young man, many in positions of authority in all countries were exercised by the reluctance of their own youth to come to terms with the realities of a developing nation. It was this aspect of day-to-day living which, both in Britain and overseas, it was felt might possibly be influenced for the better by the young speaking directly to the young.

.   .   .   .   .

Dissipation of effort could be a reason for failure: sometimes the volunteer failed to assess his own talents properly, sometimes there was just so much to do that it was extremely difficult to be sufficiently self-disciplined to establish a list of priorities, occasionally the job itself could be of such an amorphous nature as to make the imposition of any kind of pattern almost impossible.

It was particularily in youth work that this problem of dissipation flourished, and these extracts from the letters of a volunteer working in Kenya give a very good idea of the difficulties involved.

The Community Centre work was very interesting but very difficult. I was working every afternoon and evening in the different community centres. It was terribly disheartening as I felt I was never getting anywhere or making any real impact. I was running, or had a hand in, five youth clubs and boys' clubs, and only two of these had any real life to them. I asked various people about this but nobody seemed to have a constructive answer. To give an example; soon after the New Year I decided to make an all-out effort to revive one of the youth clubs with talks, debates, games, films, etc. and sent round eight hundred notices to intermediate and secondary schools in the area inviting people to come along. On the first night we had two people with whom I discussed the situation and we decided to have a film the next week, which is always a crowd-gatherer. We put a notice outside and sure enough the next week we had about forty or fifty people between the age limits we had set; and afterwards we discussed together plans and I told them what we hoped to do if we could get enough people, and we elected a small committee. Within four weeks we were down to half a dozen regular attenders who usually turned up half an hour late. I never found an answer to this problem, though I think there are many contributory causes.

I believe the only answer is to concentrate on one particular project and put the majority of your time and effort into it, with other things as secondary projects. I found I had only a limited time for visiting the boys in their homes. I feel certain that if I had done more visiting I would have been able to make the clubs more stable and increase the feeling of loyalty and the feeling that it was their club. However I am all for struggling on, for I always felt when I got very depressed and could see no concrete progress that it was worth it, if only for the relationship of friendship and understanding that was being made. I think this is especially so in this country where the majority of Africans have never known any real friendship with a European.

Except, perhaps, for the last sentence this extract could have been written of Britain instead of Kenya, and it emphasised again how small the world had become and how often its problems were the perplexities of human beings everywhere regardless of national background.

Most volunteers had periods of self-doubt, and it was right that they should. There was no room in the kind of situations that a volunteer might meet, for the self-satisfied. It was the boy who distrusted his own capacities, but yet had the courage to respond to the confidence placed in him, who ultimately did a good job. Those who felt certain that they could tackle anything and had nothing to learn were often failures.

The questions asked in moments of depression were not easy ones, or capable of simple solutions. In Thailand Alastair often queried the real reasons for his presence in the country and the motives behind his own conduct. This self-examination, common to all volunteers in some degree, was for them one of the most valuable aspects of the year. In a sense they stood outside their own normal lives, away from their family's background and country's tradition, able to question and assess without undue pressure the accepted values and taken-for-granted customs of their homeland.

I was staying with Francis for five weeks, helping him with an English course for some teachers, having already been for a tremendous trip into remote villages with some students and having stayed at many more of their homes, with the result that I had many fresh ideas and views having really seen the inside of Thailand away from Bangkok. Up to the end of term it had been fairly uphill, in perhaps a stupid way I had felt responsible for everything, and then suddenly with the holidays my mind became relaxed and the atmosphere changed as a result of the kindness of all the people I met in the provinces and the exhilarating experiences which I shared with my friends both at their homes and in the jungle. Somehow I could not help feeling why

THAI PRIEST

should I bother to try to guide them considering that I was their guest, and as they did not expect me to do it what right did I have to try to raise their ideals up to my level. Why shouldn't I just sit back, watch everything go to pot, they are happier and they think I am a kinder person, and is not this the object of the exercise. It may sound strange but these were the kind of questions that I asked myself, when I was able to reflect on my work two hundred miles away.

Part of the trouble was that no one here could see deep enough into the complexity of my position, what with luxurious surroundings, and their only remark was, 'Oh, aren't you lucky, having such nice clean buildings, etc.' with the result that I felt really alone in what I was trying to do.

That a serious concern with the deeper levels of the relationship with their students was appreciated was apparent in the greatly increased request for volunteers which came from the Thai Government at the end of this trial year.

Roger, Assistant District Commissioner in Northern Rhodesia, constantly at variance with the values he found there, yet uncertain too of where he stood himself, described in some detail the daily routine of his life. In doing so he indirectly laid bare the roots of his own uneasiness.

Whenever I walk across the Boma (the District Office), the day's complainants and the other men and women who sit waiting on the verandah for hours, and the messengers, spring to attention and salute; the latter even seemed a little shocked when I suggested it wasn't necessary. For here I'm a genuine, 100% bwana since I work for the Provincial Administration. And in order to establish personal contact with an African I have not only got to drop the officialdom myself, which isn't difficult for it's not yet ingrained, but I have also to break through what is by now the artificially inculcated instinct of respect and servility, and this latter is really difficult. I think too that my position in the government serves in a way to increase this barrier between my benevolent ambitions and myself.

Here is the story of Elijoni Kamungondo. His father moved from Kalabo district forty miles west of here on the Kalahari side of the Zambesi, to Broken Hill, where Elijoni was born. In some Boma register somewhere, however, a bored cadet or clerk wrote

165

down Kalabo as the 'home' of the Kamungondos. It didn't matter; they lived in Broken Hill and all was well. Elijoni was brought up, went to school, finished school and took a job with a printer – all at Broken Hill. Four years ago he developed a mental illness and was sent to the big mental hospital in Bulawayo, which he left after three months pronounced cured, but having lost most of his confidence and powers of self-assertion.

He resumed work in Broken Hill until six months ago he developed slight heart trouble and went into hospital again as convalescent, with a medical certificate and a note of his record, he was sent to the Boma to be forwarded to his home. The officer at the Boma thought him vague and still slightly mental, and the messengers said he was a lunatic, so his murmured comments were ignored firmly and somebody looked up his home in the register and saw Kalabo written down and made out a transport requisition to Kalabo. To Kalabo he must go.

The same thing happened at Mongu. 'Sorry chum, this letter says Kalabo.' So Mongu gives him transport over the first half of the final lap and leaves him to continue 'home' on foot – without food, money, blankets or any relatives that he knew. But at last he is alone, so he doggedly turns round and walks back 150 miles to Mankoya where he is picked up starving and given two days food from the repatriates vote, and then an officer at Mankoya gathers that he wants to go to Broken Hill, so he looks at the piece of paper and scratches his head and finally writes a letter to the District Commissioner, Mongu, saying that 'for someone supposedly mental he seems remarkable lucid about his desired destination. I suppose however that he ought to go to Kalabo since he was originally bound for there. I return him to you, trusting you will make the necessary arrangements.'

So this morning Elijoni pitches up in Mongu again. He has come by lorry but the roads are very bad and the journey has taken three days – without food, for he is in transit. As it happened the Mankoya letter came into my hands and I talked to Elijoni for half an hour this morning and got this story from him. I'm sorry to have taken so long in telling it, but the point is this – this is not an exceptional case. Everywhere there is a tendency to trust a rubber stamp in preference to a man, and this is just one instance that has involved me. At last, however, I think a little sanity may return to Elijoni's life. At least now he has food, a government rondeval to live in, and government blankets to cover him up. He is also having a thorough physical and mental check-up to make sure he can take the journey home, though I reckon that if nearly two months' lunatic shunting up and down and wandering alone have not broken him nothing ever will. I think that what impresses me most about Elijoni is the way in which he accepts things, mutely, with infinite resignation and a sort of humble dignity. Telling his story this morning he spoke no word of criticism, anger or resentment. He was in the government's hands; they would do what they though best and who was he to object?

But enough of Elijoni and my own emotional eruptions. The government knows best, (how could so vast an organisation be wrong?), and I hope I don't get too big a rocket for the letters I've just sent to Broken Hill and Mankoya.

Charlie was an apprentice volunteer working with a mission on the Aden-Yemeni border. He came from Rolls Royce's Glasgow factory and there could hardly have been a greater contrast than that between the country he came from, cool, soft, green and industrialised and the country he now found himself in, hot, barren, brown and harsh. 'The houses for the most part are built of mud bricks and look for all the world like enormous castles. The Federal Guard troop about armed to the teeth, I am told the reason is to give protection to the Emir in case any marauding Yemeni attempts to shoot him.'

Charlie was a church-goer and a staunch supporter of his Boys' Brigade, who gave him a send-off and commissioned him to look into Boys' Brigade affairs in Aden. He was slight and fair, with a soft Scottish accent and a nature that was pure gold, and he went into a difficult country to a job that was not well-defined. The request had been for a handyman for the mission hospital in the out-station of Beihan, but it troubled Charlie often that the things he found himself doing seemed to be of little importance and to have few really satisfying results.

I sometimes have doubts in my mind that I am not doing enough. Please don't misunderstand me, the trouble is I have no fixed timetable like the volunteers who teach through the day and take a youth club in the evenings. They are settled (my opinion) and have time to do something concrete, but I go from morning to morning doing anything and everything that comes my way. Example: tomorrow I have to draw the plans for the sister's bungalow as they are contemplating renovations. Previous days I have fixed up a bell for the sister, repaired a washing-machine, fixed a horn on the doctor's car, replaced a broken clutch cable, also a broken fan belt, take specimens to the government hospital and collect medical supplies, teach another of the sisters to drive.'

However, as well as all this unspectacular, though valuable, work Charlie started a youth club which was not quite like any other youth club run by any other volunteer.

I really do not know why I called it a boys' club, as the men of the town come in on the pretence of looking only, when I turn my back they are down with the boys playing blow football and snakes and ladders. All I can do is ask them to park their rifles (loaded) against the wall.

He may sometimes have felt isolated and disappointed with the size of his contribution, but Charlie did a good job. A year later, in quite another part of the world, public tribute was paid to him by a man who had seen him at work, and who told of the impression that his humble conscientiousness had made on all those with whom he came in contact.

Something of the difficulties, the doubts, the victories and the compromises which were part of the daily life of most volunteers is contained in the extracts from the correspondence of Peter, who went to Jamaica to work with the Youth Corps. Peter was serious and earnest, a firm supporter of the Salvation Army and a member of the band in which he played the trombone. He had none of the cosmopolitan and sophisticated background of one or two volunteers who had served in Jamaica before him, and he had very little experience to provide him with clues to the situations he was likely to meet. But he had absolute basic integrity and goodness of heart and these qualities stood him in good stead.

The Youth Corps was a shock at first. My introduction to it was at a camp where I stayed for a couple of days, and my first impression that of six hundred boys playing dominos, banging the pieces on their tables, creating such a noise that it stunned me. I wondered how I would ever fit in and how I could communicate with the boys – I seemed to have so little in common with them.

But gradually my feelings changed, I made my contacts in camp and began to take part in camp activities.

At first I was in charge of a squad of boys digging the foundations of a chicken house, but I found that to be rather soul-destroying and, as the boys resented the work somewhat, could not gain their confidence through that medium. I began to teach music. I have a theory lesson with two groups, and recorder classes. In addition I am trying to form a brass combination with the help of the Director of the Jamaica Military Band which has already given us some instruments. At the moment I have five boys learning the fingering of the valves on the trumpet we have.

Then I am in charge of a class of boys taking the Police Entry Examination and find the boys enthusiastic if nothing else! They study English and arithmetic and are slowly improving, but a great deal of patience and insight is needed on my part. Principles which I have taken for granted for years must be reduced to simplest terms, and one has to go over and over the same point in different ways countless times.

I tried at first to adopt a detached attitude towards the boys, but found that out of keeping with my nature, and I find I do better by being myself. I have taken a Christian stand, and have taken part in devotions more than once. The singing of the boys has made a great impression on me...

I have been Round 'C' Director since a month before Christmas. The position (I am personally responsible for about 120 of the boys in camp) can be a little irksome, but has many compensations as, for example, it brings me into closer contact with the fellows, and has increased my perceptibility so far as the camp in general is concerned. I began at a rather unfortunate time as graduation [in the West Indies, as in America, the passing-out ceremonies in any kind of institution were called graduation] was fast approaching and the boys were anxious to obtain further issues of clothing. I was continually pursued by boys who wanted to show me stained grey flannels or torn shirts. However I managed to sort things out without undue embarrassment, and feel much more confident now. I find I have to be very strict which is a pity, as I had hoped to enjoy a rather more intimate relationship with the campers. I have tried in several ways to be different from other members of staff, but the boys have long learnt to be servile and, while I know they like me, they still treat me with some restraint. I find though that my working method cannot be that of a teacher. To teach music, for instance, I have to sit down and play it with the fellows. To teach arithmetic I have to do the sums myself with the class. I have, in fact, to lead and not to drive.

I came out to Jamaica filled with the idea that I would make a great impact and put the world to rights. I realise now, however, that this is not possible. So far as Youth Corps is concerned, I may manage to effect one or two of the improvements I have in mind, but that is all. I have always felt, and feel most strongly now, that the individual is of far more importance than the institution. God makes the individual, man the institution. Youth Corps was not founded for any philanthropic motive, but to help alleviate an economic situation. It is successful in doing this. But what of the boy himself? He must benefit too. I believe that my contribution can be most effective in this sphere. It is not my desire that my name shall be blazed in gold in the annals of the Youth Corps but that some young man shall have reason to be glad I came to Jamaica.

CHAPTER V

The Strange Lands

YOUNG KENYAH

It was a tiny minority of volunteers who had ever been out of Europe before, and that small number generally consisted of youngsters whose parents had worked abroad and who had only vague memories of early childhood overseas. For most this was their first view of a larger world.

Not all were articulate about this aspect of their year abroad; many could write well about their work, their friends, their troubles, – even their thoughts and feelings, but had no words to describe the strange country in which they found themselves. Some, however, either by chance when writing about some aspect of the job, or directly compelled by the impact of scenery, customs and traditions not their own, did put into words something of the flavour of foreign lands. Necessarily these were fragments, suddenly blossoming in the midst of letters about more routine, mundane matters, and I have not tried to enlarge on them. Nevertheless, taken as a whole, they do give a glimpse of the varied world which received our volunteers and perhaps they help to give more reality to the setting in which their work was done.

In Aden, during one of the school holidays, Peter received permission from the Medical Department to go into the Protectorate

171

with a team inspecting health units. The Protectorate, the hinterland of Aden, was a wild and barren country of heat, sand and inhospitable hills, where there was always the chance of raiding across tribal frontiers or disaster from the extreme nature of the land. It was one of the latter that Peter describes.

I really had an excellent time in the Protectorate, though it all ended rather suddenly. I was doing a tour of inspection of the health units, but after a little while the car began to give us trouble until we were stuck for the night in reputedly hostile Bedouin country. Actually the Bedouin, far from being hostile, helped to push the car and even brought us food. The first vehicle that came along was next morning at 5 a.m. and, as once started we could go a little way under our own steam, this truck gave us a tug each time we stopped, but eventually broke down itself. After that a Land Rover, packed like a sardine tin with fellows evidently ready for war, that had been sent out to look for us, took the place of the lorry . . .

At last, nearing our destination, we had to descend into a river bed cast between sheer rock faces about two hundred feet high either side of us — the whole being about seventy-five yards wide.

About a quarter of an hour into this impressive wadi the rain suddenly started to come down as I have never seen rain. The driver suddenly became very scared and parked the vehicle on a piece of higher ground on the left and I, not knowing much about these things, the driver had to do some smart talking to persuade me to get out of the car and climb the rock face. I reluctantly followed him and we found an overhanging rock. Under this we sat, soaking wet and shivering cold. Suddenly a great wall of water swept down the valley making what had been a dry river bed into a raging torrent. It would have been dark by now but for the half hour long continuous flash of lightning. The noise of the thunder and the rushing water echoing between the cliff faces was something not easily forgotten.

By some miracle the car had been overturned, but had been caught in a tree, and by another miracle many of the things inside were untouched. There were dry clothes and we were immediately able to get the Primus stove working and have coffee. By another miracle all this happened in the area of a political officer who was also a first-class mechanic. The very next morning we had that car going as well as it had been before the flood. But it was not really going well enough to continue with so we were flown back in an army plane.

Bechuanaland took a number of volunteers to assist District Officers in all the multifarious duties connected with helping to govern a country which was wholly rural, vast in area, bordering on politically difficult South Africa, and inhabited by peoples whose wealth was still predominantly cattle. Ken was one of the first young men to go out to this work, and he went from a background of urban industrialisation, having lived and gone to school in one of the many growing towns close to London. Ken had considerable self-confidence and he was very articulate, both qualities which stood him in good stead when he found himself thrust into a position of increasing responsibility virtually representing the Government of Bechuanaland in vast tracts of wild country.

I have spent more time in the bush than in the offices so far, in order that I may acquire a better knowledge of the district. It is a very large one of nearly 100,000 square miles. In the bush I have been with Tsetse Fly Control all the time, except for a short hunting trip last week. With these people I have trekked into swamps on foot, with my kit on the back of an ox-drawn sleigh; walked over floating grass, a strange phenomenon which can be quite a frightening experience if one were not prepared for it. A layer of grass about a foot thick exists in certain parts of the swamps across the narrower parts of very slow-floating rivers. One can walk on it, but it ripples as does a pool when a stone is thrown in, and the thought that the water beneath the grass is usually about thirty feet deep is quite a chastening one.

On the 23rd of this month I saw my first inter-tribal squabble. There are about eight or nine tribes here, mostly small indigenous tribes, but the two main factions are invaders, so to speak.

The Batawara broke away from the Bamangwato and drove the Matabele out of Ngamiland, which is the African name for the swamps. Then the Damaras, a big tough bunch from South West Africa, came in and settled under the authority of the Batawara. They have more drive than their overlords, and are now much richer, as they are all cattle people with large herds.

Their long-standing grudge is that as they originally came, or rather were driven, from South West when the Germans were in power, it should be their right to return there. Although the Bechuanaland Government has no objection to their going, South West will not allow them entry. Consequently, although they cannot complain about our attitude towards their wishes, they are continually causing squabbles to attract attention to themselves and their plight. This particular incident occurred when two Damaras from a young regiment refused to collect wood for the kgotla. They were tried and sentenced by our rather timid and wavering Lady Regent. After sentence two hundred Damaras who had come en masse from their cattle posts (they seldom live in the village) spirited them away to hiding. After this flagrant breach of the peace the two convicted men were rearrested and jailed for the night.

The Damaras' scheme was to cause trouble over these two, assault the tribal policeman and subsequently the police when called in. This would lead to the arrest of large numbers of their group and draw attention to them; from which position of vantage they could once more air their troubles. However our spies in the camp told us of this plan and the District Commissioner persuaded them all to talk it over with him in kgotla. So we had a mass of 250 Damaras, who are really the ugliest people I have ever seen. They file their teeth and their whole aspect is one of discontent. Their only saving grace is that their women are truly lovely. They wear long, flowing, Victorian-style dresses and layer upon layer of petticoats.

Later:

At the present moment I am ensconced deep in the heart of the Kalahari Desert. The centre of the district where I am now is called Ghanzi and is situated two hundred miles south-west of Maun. Now you may have heard of Ghanzi for it is a block of European farms set up by Cecil Rhodes as a buffer between Bechuanaland Protectorate and South West Africa at the time when all countries were seizing all the land available in Africa. Apart from the farms which constitute a minute part of the district, there is a portion of 30,000 square miles to the east of Kalahari proper where the last of the wild Bushmen live in their native state.

These people, because there is no surface water in the Kalahari, go without water for seven months in the year, live unbelievably primitive lives, and are reckoned by some to be the oldest surviving race in Africa, if not in the world.

My prime reason for coming down here is to go out on a three-week survey deep into the desert, where one has to navigate with a sextant as one does at sea, and study the Bushmen with a chap who is a District Officer seconded to this work by the government mainly because of so many anti-slavery societies in U.K. and U.S.A. These societies claim that the proud, rich Hereros were chain-ganging the poor little Bushmen to herd their cattle, and that the poor white trash on the farms (and they really are poor white trash) do the same.

This is so much nonsense for no one in this world can keep a Bushman in one place, unless he puts him in chains and ties him to a tree, for these little chaps can hide so well that a bloodhound could not find them. Added to that is the fact that they can run enormous distances and they just run back to the veldt where they came from. There is one case where a Bushman went to the mines in Johannesburg and after two days ran three hundred and fifty miles back to his home in the Southern Protectorate! Another escaped from jail and although they chased him on camels it was a hundred and eighty miles before they caught him having his first drink in a village!

On this same trip I learnt to be quite an authority on drilling, for here all water is from wells or boreholes. I also increased my appreciation of cattle conditions and values as the sole industry of this country is cattle ranching. I ate my first ostrich egg, rather helped eat it as it provided breakfast for six people. I shot my first springbok and saw my first gemsbok. But above all I found myself growing to love this barren country more and more. The roads are indescribably bad, the grazing is poor in many places, there is not enough water and the government suffers from a constant lack of money, but despite all this it has a charm all its own and I am sure I will be sorry to leave. When I first came I was quite happy to stay my prescribed time and enjoy myself but I felt that any longer would be too much, no matter how absorbing the work or the people. This was not a subversive manifestation of homesickness, but a vague lack of sympathy for the country based on a want of understanding of it and its particular problems. Now this has disappeared and I am even happier than I was before, and much busier than I was before.

Later:

At the moment I am in one of the loveliest spots I have ever been in. I am in charge of the road gate on the Veterinary Cordon Fence between Ngamiland and Ghanzi district. I search all trucks passing through for meat, hides and skins, etc., in fact anything which might spread foot and mouth from Ngamiland into Ghanzi. I am eighty miles from the nearest store, one hundred and ten miles from Maun and four hundred miles from the railway line which runs up the east side of Bechuanaland Protectorate.

The daily routine is to rise at dawn, potter round mending the trucks, etc., enter in the meteorological reports, breakfast at ten, meantime searching the odd truck which comes through, no lunch, it is too hot, drink innumerable cups of coffee when the fence patrols come in; write letters, read, hunt for meat for the fence labourers on the other side of the stock free zone, work out the mileage for the salary claims, dinner and bed at eight. In all it's early to bed, early to rise, something I've never done before, and I feel much better for it. The food tends to be mealy meal and meat for every meal, just what the Africans eat, so I am living the very same life exactly at the moment; and no wonder they live to a ripe old age and stay quite well preserved.

Later:

Since I last wrote I have undergone one of the biggest tests of my short career. I wrote at that time from the cordon fence where I was keeping out the foot and mouth. Well I stayed there a full month, then returned to Ghanzi for a week. Then believe it or not, I went back for yet another month of solitude. When I say solitude I mean that although I saw people passing through I spent the vast majority of my time alone. There were times of complete inactivity such as when my lamp broke. Then in the evening I could not read, nor was I tired enough to go to sleep. At such times the temptation to leap up a tree and yodel at the moon was at its greatest. But, although I would not care to undergo such a long period of isolation again, I have the great satisfaction of knowing that I could if I had to, and still suffer no great discomfort.

This is a hard country and I revel in the fact that, so far, I have been hard enough to take everything which it has to offer in my stride. Everything from shooting, gutting, cleaning and cooking my own meat, through dust, sand, heat and sweat, hours of driving on the worst roads in Africa (that fact is not exaggerated), talking to a Bushman murderer who waters my garden and whose nose and mouth are completely eaten away by syphilis, without flinching, to explaining diplomatically to a hysterical European woman that she has committed an offence and that if she does not pay up she will go to court. All these things and many more serve as indications to me what sort of a person I am.

This is probably the experience of every volunteer and nothing new, but I am finding myself quicker here than I would ever do in the U.K. I have already achieved an attitude of mind which is so much more adult than when I left, that I am sure it would have taken several years at university to achieve the same result. This is partly because the society here is purely adult, but mainly because I am doing a man's work and if one does not quickly acquire an adult method of approaching it one is liable to be dismissed as an upstart child. I see, now that the daze of newness and mystery has cleared completely from all around me, just how valuable an experience this is, and know that it is making a new person of me. Rather it is that I am discovering qualities in me that I never knew existed.

British Honduras suffered a severe hurricane shortly after the third lot of volunteers had arrived and settled in. So terrible was the wind that a large part of the town of Belize was destroyed. For the volunteers, two boys and two girls, this was the most frightening as well as, perhaps, the most exhilarating experience of their lives. In a sense every volunteer longed for a natural disaster, because it was in this situation that he knew himself to be urgently and wholly needed.

This particular hurricane, Hattie, passed the Cayman Islands in the West Indies on its way to Belize. Fortunately for the islands the real force of the wind veered away from them, but here too there was a trail of fear and catastrophe. Michael in British Honduras and Ian in the Caymans both wrote about their experiences.

Ian first, as the Caymans were in the path of the hurricane on its way to Belize.

You probably did not know that the eye of the storm came

177

within sixty miles of Cayman, and it was heading straight for us when it turned abruptly by some quirk of fate and hit British Honduras fair and square.

It was frightening enough here in Cayman, as the storm was due to hit us at midnight on Sunday in the darkness! The Sunday was a hectic day, spent in securing the buildings of the inhabitants. The number of sheets of corrugated iron that I hammered over the windows must run into hundreds. It had been raining constantly for almost two days and all we wore were shorts — and I can tell you the heavy tropical rain is very cold. By darkness on Sunday everyone had retreated to their houses — and most of them are flimsy wooden structures unable to withstand anything — to sit up and await the worst. I have never seen real fear before as I saw it then and the six hours vigil until midnight was purgatory. The winds in gusts were over 100 m.p.h. and the seas were gigantic and came right across up to the house. It was not at first obvious that the storm had turned aside, as there was no electricity and no radio communication, and we thought it was the lull before the storm.

Our house was full of 'old folk', all of them over sixty, and they were quite petrified and never once spoke during the night. By morning it was obvious that the worst had missed us but even so the damage was amazing. The island is saucer-shaped and the central portions are vast swamp areas which become flooded by heavy rains. The roads were undermined and under water too, and all the electric cables were down. Beach property suffered tremendous damage too. The total rainfall for a period of forty-eight hours was sixteen and a half inches, so you can understand the situation.

And in Belize Michael was helping to cope with the aftermath of the storm's full fury.

As you will have heard, the damage in many parts of Belize was really quite extensive. As most of the buildings are wooden, many of them were destroyed completely. The others were all damaged, some fairly lightly, others so badly that they will have to come down. There was, and still is, mud and debris everywhere, and the whole of Belize was at one stage submerged in ten feet of water. The wind also took everything everywhere. Part of the roof of the Governor's house, which is a good half mile from us, eventually landed up in the road only a few yards away from our house. One house, which was a few blocks away from us, floated, complete, in our direction: we watched it sail gracefully down, turn the corner, and finally come to rest on the other side of the road from us, in perfect position so that when the water went down the front door led on to the pavement! It was only missing its floor, and was quickly occupied next day by a family who had lost their house completely; the only trouble was that the ground where it settled happened to be a disused grave-yard, and they had to contend with one or two rather ancient gravestones as their furniture! Our house stood well, although the bottom filled with water and we can only live in the top.

I had a job of house-to-house visiting in a certain area. I was meant to find out all particulars of families living in each house, so that the Red Cross could then be able to distribute clothes and mattresses more fairly and to those who were considered by the visitor to be really in need. This proved a never-ending job — mine was an area which was almost entirely washed away, so that immediately after the hurricane there were no more than five houses standing. However people were putting up little shacks, etc., to live in so fast that by the time I started there were liter-ally over eighty 'houses' up already — and of course every day another family would move in. In the end we covered the area three times, and even then we weren't satisfied — so I tried to do it a fourth time just before school began, but time ran out be-fore I could finish. Some were really in need of the clothing and mattresses they received and were truly thankful for them; others, I'm afraid, rather took it as an opportunity for getting more clothes free. Of course not everybody could be given a mattress and there was some amount of resentment amongst a few of those who did not receive one, I was continually visited by people who thought they had been missed out, and who wanted me to give them a paper to get a mattress. It was hard to turn most of them away, and to explain, without their being offended, why I could not give them one . . .

Edwin was the first volunteer to go to Fiji, and during his year he was the only volunteer in that country. He also had another dis-tinction, he was taken out of school in the last week of the summer term, with the willing co-operation of his headmaster, and put straight on to a Royal Naval Auxiliary vessel bound for Suva.

This passage, a very valuable one from our point of view, was offered suddenly, by telephone, a few days before the ship left. Edwin, who was destined for Fiji, was still at school and we were hesitant as to how he, himself, his headmaster and his parents would greet the proposal to remove him at short notice and launch him on a seven weeks' sea journey. After some discussion it was decided that the chance of a lift all the way to Fiji, a chance which would not be repeated, could not be lost and a series of telephone calls were put through to the grammer school where Edwin was still a pupil, and to his mother. The result was one of wholehearted co-operation; Edwin, a Queen's Scout, was ready to move at once, and seventy-two hours later he was packed and ready and on the high seas.

He went to teach in the large government secondary school in Suva, the capital of Fiji. For him it was, in many ways, an idyllic year the heart and core of which lay in his visits during the holidays to the villages of some of his pupils. One such visit is described here.

After life in a city living in a village was extremely refreshing. It was a village of outstanding beauty, set behind a long coral and sand beach fringed with lofty palms, overshadowed by green mountains, blue sea, white surf on its coral reef, hot sunshine and children playing in the water complete the picture — real South Seas! Food: taro, tapioca, breadfruit, yams, roasted bananas (all starchy), sea urchin, shellfish, sea slug, fish, wild spinach, taro leaves (cooked in coconut milk) and turtle's head (by custom always presented to the chief's house where I was staying).

For three weeks I ate no meat, saw no European, didn't sit in a chair, drank no milk, ate no bread and butter, read no newspaper, heard no radio — quite a change from city life. At first I found it hard to sit cross-legged on the floor to eat meals — but my legs soon became accustomed to the unusual position. The hospitality was wonderful. Not only did my hosts provide huge quantities of food, but custom demands that the other villagers bring to a house where a guest is staying huge dishes laden with food. When a family is eating and someone passes outside, he must be invited in to eat — he inevitably declines.

New Year is still being celebrated with much throwing of water and mud, much chasing over palm trunk bridges in the hope of causing the quarry to fall into the water, much beating of tree-trunk drums and roaming the village by night singing beautiful Fijian songs – always in harmony never in unison. I worked a little in the padi fields and spent some of the time in slinging mud. I took some of the boys camping in the bush and learnt many new techniques. We walked half a mile to a deep part of the stream to bath – yes bath! The trouble was that heavy rain made the path muddy and having cleaned ourselves in the stream, returning to the village without getting dirty again was a considerable problem. I did plenty of swimming and was made to look like a beginner by even the youngest of the village boys.

To anyone who entertains a feeling of superiority over black people I would say, 'Live in a Fijian village for a week. I guarantee that you will realise just how inferior you really are.' Everything we did the Fijians did far better than I – at times I felt quite melancholy as I realised that I can never achieve what they do in the things that lead to true happiness – music, rhythm, toughness, endurance, self-amusement, self-reliance, confidence, cheerfulness, swimming, diving, climbing, walking. At present I would willingly give up my British heritage to be a Fijian boy living in a village. I have nothing but admiration and hero-worship, blended with a little envy for the Fijian teenagers – in the villages.

Travel within the country could be the source of many interesting experiences. Volunteers always travelled third class, or by lorry, or occasionally by bicycle or even elephant, not so much because they had very little extra money as because they automatically associated themselves with the level of society which travelled in this way.

In India the Johns made several long journeys by train, and their description of this way of journeying would be true of other countries in Asia and Africa.

The way to make friends – and enemies – is to travel third class on the Indian Railways. I hope I shall never again have the privilege of being wedged with thirty-four other unfortunates and their luggage in a very small third class compartment. There was a bit of a fight at one station when sixteen got in, and from there for three hundred miles the doors did not

SIKH
open again. They used the windows. But in spite of

discomforts we had a really worthwhile time. It is a bit humiliating to be told by someone you thought an illiterate villager that television travels in straight lines not waves; especially when you were not sure yourself and so could not correct him.

One was also struck by the amazing knowledge of the world so often shown in the people we met. A communist in Kerhala left me wishing I had never opened my big mouth.

Holiday expeditions could give glimpses of wild and strange country in the remote parts of any territory. In Kenya Tony joined an expedition going several hundred miles up the Tana river. Kenya had at this time a National Service force known as the Kenya Regiment Training Corps. Every six months there was a training course for 'Kenya Youth' (European), and at the end of these courses a safari, or expedition, was arranged. On this particular expedition there were eleven boys, including Tony, an officer and a sergeant.

The expedition was wonderful – really exciting and full of interest and most worthwhile. We travelled about two hundred miles down river in stone-age dug-outs, a most dangerous craft I can assure you, as they tip over almost without provocation. However our canoes were two of these trees lashed together side by side, and so we were quite stable – a little too stable I'm afraid – had they been any more stable they wouldn't have gone at all, so heavy were they.

There was nothing military about the expedition at all – except for sleeping bags, 'mossie' nets and other equipment. It was most exciting and many were our adventures. Several times canoes overturned on hidden logs, spilling their occupants and kit into the crocodile and hippo infested waters – which is no exaggeration – there are thousands of these creatures in the river. Game was everywhere – lion, elephant, buffalo, giraffe, rhino, gazelle, antelope, buck and hippo, and croc too. About the only thing missing were kangaroos! And it wouldn't have surprised me in the least to have a couple, such a fantastic, wonderful, beautiful place is the Northern Frontier District. Many times we saw elephant and on one occasion were charged by a large bull while actually on the river. That was quite a thing. We were also chased by hippo, who tried to overturn the canoes by rising with them on their backs – fortunately we managed to keep just ahead, with the hippos rising up just a few feet behind, and becoming angrier and angrier.

There could hardly have been a more different mood or setting than that of James, teaching with a mission in Labrador, one of the very few to be working outside the tropics.

All the trouters have gone north, and the village is very empty. I spend my time tending the mission trout net and smoke house, and we are preparing the boat for some coastal trips. I have already been on one three-day trip north with the store manager, to take salt to the nearer trouters, who had a hard time getting through the pack-ice. We only met one bad patch, and I must say that I enjoyed the experience; the ice is contorted sometimes into fantastic shapes, and the cracks are a bluey, bright green. The coast has some magnificent scenery, with a surprising variety of colour, and the tiny camps of the fishermen looked lost and forlorn, clinging to the foot of great steep hills.

We visited two deserted settlements en route — Okak, once the largest Moravian station on the coast, wiped out by a flu epidemic in 1919, and Nutak, abandoned in 1948 as the population moved south. The houses at Nutak still stand, and it was strange to browse through the things left behind — old diaries, books and so on. The weather on the first two days was very hot, but — and this is typical of Labrador — on our second night out the wind changed right round and started to blow a gale. We had to change anchorage at 1 a.m., and then sail back to Nain to wet, cold and fog.

In Malaya Sari left the Blind School in Penang, which is an island, and went across to the mainland for a short holiday. An extremely friendly girl, Sari quickly recovered from any nervousness she may have felt about travelling alone in a strange land and settled down to enjoy all she saw and make the most of her travelling companions.

At present I am having a week's holiday in Perak about fifty miles from Penang. I am staying in an attap house in a Malay kampong. The occupants of this house are three missionaries. This is very different from Penang. So very peaceful surrounded by homely sights and sounds. The sound of the axe as it cracks into wood, the sound of the wind in the rubber trees, the muffled and indistinct noises of people going about the task of living.

Through my bedroom window I can see Che Miriam in her sarong and kabaya seeing to the washing hanging on the line. On another line are hanging the sheets of latex. The time is just after three o'clock. It is hot and most people are resting in their houses.

I came here on the fifth from Penang. Someone drove me down to the ferry and from there I went by myself. The ferry left at 8.15 a.m. Already the sun was very bright. I saw what I thought was a porpoise plunging up and down through the water. There were quite a number of boats anchored off-shore with strange names like Jag Jawa and Warszawa. I had been given instructions how to get to Selama, so when I got off the ferry I asked for one seat in a taxi to Kulim. After a lot of shouting among the taxi drivers I was led to a taxi and put in the front seat. A few minutes later a Chinese man, plus newspaper, climbed in the back. The driver jumped in and off we rattled, but not far because our car turned off the road into a kampong and stopped outside a shop. I had a sudden desire to laugh because I was so reminded of Elspeth Huxley. In her books of her travels in Africa she continually tells of rattling rides in taxis with strange companions.

Out of the shop emerged a Malay family. An old Malay man climbed into the taxi. The family didn't seem particularly perturbed about his going. I think they were more interested in my presence in the car! Off we went at full speed to Kulim. Whenever a car appeared on the horizon the driver pressed his hand on the horn as hard as he could and left it there till the vehicle was disappearing towards the horizon.

At Kulim the Chinese man disappeared. The only sound I had heard from him during the journey was the folding of newspaper followed by a yawn approximately every twenty minutes. The little Malay man and myself were shown another taxi into which we got. Our new driver was a very careful driver.

The thing that impressed me most about the journey were the rubber trees. Line upon line with diagonal scars across their bark and the little cup attached to catch the latex. We passed many reminders of the Emergency. Barbed wire fences surrounding the lines and new villages. Though officially the Emergency is over the threat of communism is ever present. I've heard it said that while vast sums of money were being spent on jungle warfare, the real propaganda was going on in the Chinese schools.

Roger, in Northern Rhodesia, angry and upset by much of what he saw and did, wrote at length about the incidents of his daily life, perhaps because this helped in some measure to assuage his uneasiness and clarify his own judgements. Roger was an extremely intelligent young man and he wrote with a poetic perception which indicated the success he might have been had he found himself in a country where he had the freedom to follow his own sympathetic involvement. He was also loyal, in so far as was possible, both to the government which he temporarily served and to the organisation which sent him, occasionally conflicting loyalties which contributed something to his unease. I believe, however, that there was an even deeper, perhaps unrecognised, conflict within Roger himself. By temperament and background he was the kind of young man who, a few years before, would have accepted the life of a cadet in the Administrative Service of Northern Rhodesia as a normal way of life. Now he was aware of the narrowness of its horizons when viewed from a newer and larger world and he rebelled against its paternalistic philosophy; but his instinct had not yet caught up with his intelligence and he found it difficult to resolve the schism within himself.

The incidents described in this extract sound very strange in the context of modern Britain, but they were everyday occurences in the life of a government servant in Northern Rhodesia.

Yesterday I was with the District Officer when he interrogated a witch, a small, old, ugly woman with a most extraordinary deadness in her face, a sort of bovine apathy of infinite patience, infinite stupidity, and total unawareness of the world around her which combined to make her the least human human I have ever seen. I had the feeling that if I stuck a spear in her or offered her £1,000 she still would not move a muscle. But when we got her into the office she gave us quite a lucid account of what she had done — killed the baby of a neighbour which she was looking after, buried it, dug it up three days later and eaten the heart and testicles hanging up the rest of the flesh to dry as biltong. The policeman who arrested her had thoughtfully brought in the skull and some of the biltong for our inspection, but they had been badly prepared and the skull stank, while the flesh crumbled into a fine powder and blew all over the office. The reason for it all was that she was getting old and didn't like it. At the end of her statement my feeling was one of complete helplessness — I just don't know what you start to do for a wretched creature like that. Clearly she wasn't fully responsible for her actions — the idea conveys nothing to her, words convey nothing to her, punishment is the same.

This helplessness I mentioned is not an unfamiliar sensation. Occasionally I help the Clerk of the Court and we sit in a large air-conditioned room, and the District Commissioner sits on a platform behind us, and people come in one after the other and stand in a box, and the public prosecutor stands up and says what the man has done, and after each point the District Commissioner asks the man if he admits it to be true and the man says 'yes' and everything goes very smoothly, and then at the end the District Commissioner asks the man why he did it, and a sort of uneasy blankness descends on the room and there is silence. So the man is sent to prison for four months and the blankness never leaves his face and we scribble down the sentence in the space for it on the blue form and tick off the case number and so on to the next.

Some of the legal business around here, actually, is the one thing that angers me at times. The Clerk of the Court has as part of his duties to serve writs on debtors and, if no money is forthcoming, to sell them out. In fact he is as lenient as he can possibly be but even so he has frequently to walk into a man's house, pile every moveable object in it on to a lorry and drive it away. I have accompanied it once or twice and heard him explain to the owner the way in which a £1 debt has increased to £9 through solicitor's costs, and how solicitors can't be kept waiting. 'Solicitors have to live, the same as other people.' And the wretched little debtor, who earns 35/- a month as a garden boy, stands and watches his miserable tin basins and his blanket and sleeping mat vanishing on to the big green lorry. He is not even angry, he's just completely bewildered by the whole thing. He has owed £1 and he supposes it's fair enough in the end that he pays it back and indeed he has offered £1 and it has been taken, but still, it seems, he is in debt to a man in Lusaka whose name he doesn't know, who earns £200 per month and will spend the miserable pittance obtained from the sale of the tin basins on a dinner in town with his wife, or perhaps on a gramaphone record, or perhaps on a bottle of Drambuie. Looked at in terms of income £9 to the garden boy is the equivalent of £1,200

to the solicitor; in terms of total worldly wealth it is considerably more. And how has this solicitor earned the authority to wield this amazing justice, disregarding apparently all human values in the name of so high an ideal? He has passed an examination in London thirty years ago.

I'm sorry to wax so vehement on the subject, but it has made a very strong impression on me.

Occasionally I stroll out on to the plain before going to bed and the sights and sounds and smells that follow the fantastic sunsets really defy description: the vast moonlit infinity of the plain studded with weird, surrealist trees: the sky, silver and vivid with stars and the myriad fireflies flashing green on the ground: the almost inperceptible breeze brings snatches of distant drums and the heavy fragrance of the mango trees fringing the hill: the crickets hum away incessantly on three distinct notes like three harmonised electric buzzers – the continuo to the booming of the froggy chorus with its deafening Wagnerian crescendos and the wistful, Brahmsian diminuendos: quite regardless of the concert the big barble bubble and splash in the canals, and the grass rustles secretively and the reeds turn into snakes and then back into reeds so that your heart béats slowly again. I understand better every day the people who have been 'bitten with Africa' and can't stay away: I'm being bitten too, and not simply by mosquitoes.

In North Borneo another Roger struggled also with a difficult environment. This was the Chinese school in which Sean and Fred had encountered so many vicissitudes and Roger was, in fact, one of their predecessors. For him it had been entirely fresh ground, he was one of the first batch of volunteers to be sent to North Borneo, and therefore there was no background of helpful information from another's experiences. It was Roger and his companion who had to fight for the acceptance of strangers in the school, from which struggle Sean and Fred, though they might not have realised it, benefited. And their efforts were complicated by a bitter internal conflict between the two volunteers themselves, always a hazard when sending a pair to a hard, isolated project.

Roger's description of the situation in the little town of Tenom is a good background to the job and its extra commitments as portrayed earlier by Fred and Sean.

This is a very small town, completely isolated from the rest of North Borneo, except for a single line railway track linking it to the capital and an earth road linking it to the biggest town in the interior. The town population here is overwhelmingly Chinese and the country population is a mixture of poor Chinese farmers and natives working on the rubber estates. There is a very sharp division between town and country populations — what might be called class distinction. The town people despise the country people even amongst the same nationalities. Perhaps despise is too hard a word to use, but there is definitely a feeling of superiority amongst the town people and one of inferiority amongst the villagers.

All the people have one thing in common, they are intent on amassing as much wealth as they can in as short a time as possible For this reason they make bad rubber planters as they tap the rubber when it is too young and then proceed to bleed the tree ruthlessly to death. Like human beings anywhere their characters are full of inconsistencies. They will break their backs to scrape up a bit of capital from their few acres of land and then in one night they will gamble it away. Gambling is their only entertainment except for the cinema and drinking.

The Chinese on the whole are not heavy drinkers, but the natives are, although they rarely have enough money to drink anything but 'tapai'. Education is extremely important to the Chinese and this is the first place outside the capital to have senior education. Discipline in the Chinese schools is too good to be true, but in the mission school there are deceptive signs of life. I say deceptive as they usually get channelled into uncooperativeness, when the students realise that what you are teaching them is not strictly part of the syllabus. The root of the trouble is that in the mission school the students are too old for primary school (some are twenty-two) and many of them are settled into family business and they do not stand to gain anything materially from their education. However this only applies to the two oldest classes who are the last of these children prevented from having an education at an earlier age by the war.

The town and country distinctions seem to get fairly healthily ironed out at school where games, intellectual ability and character play a more important part. The Chinese boys are fond of sports like any English boy and are good sportsmen, except when playing in competition and feeling it necessary to save face. The town boys play more regularly than the country as they have not so far to travel and are not expected to help with manual work.

The problem of the young intelligentsia here is not as acute as in the capital since further education is a comparatively recent innovation and there is still considerable rural influence. Last year was the first year that the school had any graduates who had finished three years senior education. These graduates have either become primary school teachers (one a headmaster), stayed at home to help the family, or gone to university in Formosa. In two year's time the school is going to take an Oxford and Cambridge Board exam. What the students who pass this are going to do I don't know. I expect they will be able to gain scholarships for further education and come back as engineers or teachers ready to help with the development of their country. Those who fail and those who don't complete their education will be the problem. They will have only one choice and that will be to return to the land, either farming or rubber tapping on the big estates. The future happiness of the country will depend on whether this can be accomplished without any feelings of disillusion or degradation.

Perhaps I have gone far enough with my picture. Now I will explain how I fit into it. When I arrived here I was full of wonderful ideas and high ideals. I was going to change the face of the earth. My first step and my first fall was perhaps the hardest. I tried to start a football team and train them. I failed to start a team, but I learnt a lot in the process. What I learnt is not to try to force anything down anyone's throat. Let them taste it first and if they like it they'll come back for more. The Chinese will

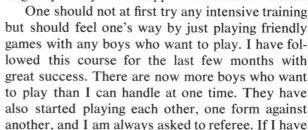

give you plenty of verbal support, but to get them to give you any active support is a different matter.

One should not at first try any intensive training but should feel one's way by just playing friendly games with any boys who want to play. I have followed this course for the last few months with great success. There are now more boys who want to play than I can handle at one time. They have also started playing each other, one form against another, and I am always asked to referee. If I have

DOCK WORKER, NORTH BORNEO

enough time next term I want to form a committee to take control when I leave. My ambition will be realised when they can lose without a fight and ill-feeling.

Not all the time, however, was spent wrestling with the problems of the job; there were idyllic interludes too. One of the girl volunteers in North Borneo described the setting of a school camp.

The camp site is ideal — a silver beach, clear green water, a beautiful coral reef and a shaded area with a number of attap huts to sleep in. We were in charge of the girls, and helped with the cooking. Our kitchen was another little attap hut hung about with bananas and pineapples and we cooked luscious curry meals over open fires. Some of the boys caught a python one day and we ate that — very tasty, and they regularly caught fresh fish, all beautifully coloured. It seemed a shame to kill them. We spent most of our time in the water looking at the coral and fish through masks, and also made an expedition into the jungle which was quite exciting: we drank water from some of the creepers which the native boys cut down for us — very sweet and clear.

North Borneo's next door neighbour was Sarawak, and here, whatever the situation in which they worked, most volunteers had the chance to see something of the interior, the country up the long rivers — which are the highroads of Sarawak — where live the Dayaks, the Ibans, the Kenyahs, Kayans and Kelabits.

Some, like Graham, actually worked in a community development scheme with Ibans. There was a strange exotic ring about his description of his living quarters.

This is as far as the pink-painted Chinese launch can reach and there is a long, low storehouse here with a kitchen behind it and set in the rubber plantation on the hill are the schoolroom (perfectly adequate) and the boarding-house (some boarding-house!) with my small room on top containing one bed on floor; mosquito net; small table; very small chair; door which just shuts and corrugated iron roof so that when the heavens are opened it sounds like a band of enraged angels beating with all their angelic might above your head — sleep is then impossible and of course the rain comes in. I seem to revel in it!

And later, when he had temporarily changed his station to help out elsewhere he wrote:

Terrible journey; barefooted walking or struggling up mountains and streams, along mud-clotted paths, up hills, down hills, through pouring rain, under skin-blistering heat. Stayed a night in a very backward longhouse. Reminded me, if that is possible, of Stone Age pagans with open fires, just rice to eat, loin clothes, long hair, pounding the padi (rice)

BORNEO HOUSE

and threshing it with their feet. No mosquito nets, and thousands of sand flies which caused a sleepless night. No time for more; am still happy despite all.

Or there was the other Ian, whose work was with the Youth Officer in the capital. Because of accommodation difficulties Ian lived in the Teacher Training Centre, sleeping in the dormitory with the trainees. In the bed next to him was a Kayan boy whose home was up the longest river in the north of Sarawak, the Baram. Ian and the Kayan lad struck up a warm friendship, and when the holidays came he was asked to go home to the longhouse with Maing, to meet his people and find out how they lived.

A Kayan village consisted of one long house, built on stilts on the river bank. Each family had a room in the house. (In assessing the population of any one longhouse it was usual to ask how many doors it had. Behind each door lived one family unit.) Down the whole length of the front of the house ran a wide verandah which was both the village street and the communal meeting-place in the evenings. Each house had a chief, who had his room in the centre of the house and who held himself responsible for the welfare and welcome of guests.

During my expedition to the Baram I lived with the Kayans and Kenyahs for about one month, and for two weeks I stayed in one longhouse where I lived like a Kayan.

I went hunting, fishing, fruit gathering and adapted myself to their way of life.

Probably as a result of this I was formally adopted by the longhouse, with much ceremony, singing and dancing; and my

192

Kayan name is Lejan Sungei Batu. After my adoption I was afforded great privileges, taken to their tombs which they are forbidden to visit themselves.

There is a story attached to every day spent in the longhouse. The dancing, especially of the Kayans, is exceedingly graceful and I was taught how to dance by my Kayan friend at whose house I was the guest. He is now my blood brother.

The bonds between myself and the longhouse are not temporary, but for life. Maing, my 'brother' will help me to write in Kayan to the people of his longhouse, and the link will be kept through writing to him in English when I leave.

My Kayan father took me everywhere with him, and he gave me the best advice any person of one culture mixing with another could receive. His words were: 'We are very happy for you to come and stay with us and live our way of life, but some of our customs must seem strange to you. If you are asked to do anything or eat anything that is against your beliefs do not do it and do not eat it. You are my son, but my son from a different world to life here on the Baram.' Words of wisdom I think. It was with great reluctance that I left the longhouse to return to Kuching.

Much further east, in the Pacific Ocean, lay the Solomon Islands. Most volunteers bound for this part of the world carried with them exotic mental pictures which were confounded by the reality. Certainly they seemed to come into contact with a higher incidence of disease than volunteers elsewhere, and those who suffered from malaria found it to be a particularly virulent type. Very early on one wrote outspokenly:

> The first thing I discovered was that the stories about tropical South Sea Island paradises are indubitably rubbish. What with mosquitoes (disease-spreading), scorpions, sharks, centipedes (sometimes a foot long), giant sting-rays (twelve feet across) not to mention snakes and poisonous leaves in the bush, these islands are not the healthiest place in the world.

> Before he left his mother had confided in me that she was glad to have her son so well away from the possibility of a nuclear bomb. I used sometimes to

CARRYING BASKET, SARAWAK

remember this and wonder if she realised how much greater were the actual risks to which he was exposed! There were other hazards too.

The past month here in the islands there has been one earth tremor and several storms; these have resulted in damage to many coastal villages near here. I was therefore called out on March 25th to take food and medicine to a village that had been totally destroyed. It necessitated a walk of nearly two hours along the coast and I arrived to find that the people had fled to the bush. Their houses had been covered completely by sand and many coconut palms had been brought to the ground, adding to the damage by falling upon several canoes that the villagers had been forced to leave when they fled. The sea, it appeared, had swept over the protecting reef barrier three times the previous evening, with a suddenness akin to a tidal wave, it had reached some three hundred yards inland and had left fish and shellfish by the score when it had retreated. There was, however, little physical suffering done to the people beyond a few coughs and colds, so I distributed some aspirin and departed taking with me two lobsters.

That was Niven who, when he realised that he would be expected to be ready to give injections, taught himself to do so by practising on an orange. Angus came across traces of more dangerous times now, astoundingly, taking their place as tales for an inexperienced generation. In this case a garden was really a cultivated piece of land in the surrounding bush and not the neat patch attached to an inhabited building that is more common in Britain.

Last week, when I was in the garden working and talking with my boys the conversation began to turn on the subject of war. As we were on the point of leaving for home I asked them if there had been any fighting on the actual ground where we were standing. They replied by leading me to the top of a near-by hill which forms part of the actual garden ground. After they had hacked around in the bush for some time, one of them suddenly let out a great yell and of course I dashed across immediately to see what his find was. I was not disappointed when he proudly showed a skeleton. He said it must have been a Jap because the Americans came and took away all their dead. On picking up the skull I found a large hole surrounded by many cracks about an inch above his right eye. Closer inspection revealed he had exceptionally bad teeth; poor fellow.

Chris, working as an Assistant District Officer, found himself with an interesting job.

Since the New Year I've been staying among the Gilbertese who've been settled here, the aim being to investigate their feeding habits. The Solomons are so entirely different to the Gilberts that the government were a little anxious about what they were doing for food. It is difficult to get to know without living with them, because the inflexible custom is to give visitors the best food – tinned pilchards and rice.

They proved very co-operative, and always gave me the same food as they would normally be eating, and so cross-legged on a mat I tore pieces of baked fish off, trying not to notice that the head and tail were there, left on as the tastiest part. The main difficulty of living with people existing chiefly on fish was to try and live through their day-long fishing trips. Hot sun is bad enough working in the shade, but in an open canoe it can cause great damage to one's skin; was it tender afterwards?! That particular expedition was a shark hunt, but we had no takes.

Chris had fair-reddish hair and the agonies of sunburn must have been an ordeal for him.

In the middle of their year in Somaliland Peter and David faced a unique crisis. Independence was coming, but it had not occurred either to them or to us that this would make any difference in their position. They operated, after all, on a very humble, non-political level and, whatever the state of the country, teachers would always be needed.

A week or so before Independence, however, we were disconcerted to receive a cable from the British authorities in Hargeisa requesting us to remove the volunteers as, by and large, the British were leaving the territory. This was a difficult situation; our instinct was to have the boys stay on so long as they were wanted by the new Somali Government, but we did not know clearly what the position within the country actually was. So a cable went off to Peter and David asking them to tell us whether they wished to stay and if it were possible for them to do so. Very quickly the reply came back: on no account did they want to leave at what they felt might be the vital moment when their services would be most badly needed because of the shortage of teachers.

Satisfied with this assurance we went ahead at once with arrangements to accredit them to the new government, which gratefully accepted the offer of their services, and to see that their sustenance and pocket-money would continue to be provided. When the British moved out Peter and David remained behind.

They described this experience at some length in their letters.

As you already know the country is to obtain Independence next month. However what few people at home will know is that a grand 'exodus' is taking place and within a month only about eighty people (European I mean) will still be here, none of whom, so far as we can discover, will be remaining after December this year. It is, to use a simple metaphor, a 'wholesale sellout', and as far as the majority are concerned the attitude is 'you want it, you can have it' and 'the sooner we are out the happier everyone will be . . .'

Last week we were told simply, 'You must be out of the country by the 24th June,' by the Director of Education. As far as we know this is only because there will be no money to continue our upkeep, and we have requested that he enquires of this so that we may remain. At present we are awaiting a telegram to give us the news, we are hoping that we shall be able to continue. But as with everything else all we can do is carry on and wait . . .

Later:

Greetings from the Somali Republic! Nothing seems more natural to us than to stay on, and the Independance Celebrations were a sight to remember. We managed to get into Hargeisa during the holiday where the celebrations were naturally the most colourful and vociferous. I suppose their pattern must have been much the same as those in other 'emergent' countries this year and next and at this stage in history generally.

There were the formalities of the departure of the Governor, beating of the retreat, and of the official handing over of the army to the Somalis. After this latter ceremony the soldiers marched through the town followed by a surging mass of what must have been scores of thousands of Somalis shouting, 'Honolato, Honolato', 'Long live, Long live'. A sight never to be forgotten and one which demonstrated the force and dynamic appeal of nationalism.

We were more deeply impressed by the Somali celebration in Hargeisa on the eve of Independence which began after sunset on June 25th. Independence or no Independence we always seem to do differently from the rest of the European population and this occasion was no exception. We found ourselves lone 'white men' amongst twenty thousand Somalis and spent the first hour or so lurking in the shadows glancing over our shoulders looking for possible assassins, but when our presence was known we were invited to ringside seats. From here we were able to watch the various political parties entertain the crowd with singing from a makeshift stage among the trees, or, more accurately, the thorny scrub. The highlight of the singing was undoubtedly a particular song which had not been sung in public before in which a man, one of my former pupils at the Trades School, and three seductive women, expounded on the emancipation of women. Whilst it is difficult to appreciate the subtleties of a foreign language the mannerisms of the performers and, more important, the reaction of the audience conveyed all that was necessary.

Even so the women still fetch water, erect the houses, herd the sheep and camels, and generally exist for the men's convenience.

Naturally there was a tremendous atmosphere of excitement and expectancy as midnight neared. The least incident provoked a surge of restless exhilaration to pass through the remarkably disciplined crowd. It cannot be denied that before Independence there were definite signs of hostility especially from the townspeople, but there were no such signs on this occasion at all. One cannot help feeling that the Somalis celebrated Independence with the British and not in spite of them.

It is good to think that at least two young Britons celebrated with them.

What was it like, this country which, in spite of it harshness, its intermittent hostility and its unpredictable temper, became almost a second home to Peter and David, so that long after their return they maintained contacts with many of its people?

Only yesterday at school I stood watching hundreds (literally I think four hundred must have passed the school in ten or fifteen minutes) of camels being driven to the river bed to be watered, but not one of them was being ridden. The Somalis just do not seem to ride the camels, they must prefer to walk. I say that the camels (sheep and goats) are being taken to the river to be watered but do not misunderstand me, they do not drink water from the river, there has not been any in it since before we arrived! In the river bed one can find hundreds of wells, it looks just like a very accurate heavy bombing raid. These wells are dug by the inhabitants of Hargeisa (they take two days to dig, are about thirty feet deep, but only the diameter of an ordinary dustbin) who sell water to the animal owners who come from fifty miles around to water the animals; standard rate at present is fifteen cents, about twopence, per camel. This year however water is very cheap as last year was a good summer, which means here that there was plenty of rain. The previous year there was very little rain and a year ago water was so short that it was necessary for the government to help by taking water to the interior. Then water from the wells was costing 1/- per gallon bucket. Just think of it, 3/- a day to wash pots, something like 7/6 for a bath, etc.

The Somalis avoid both these particular things. They burn food from their utensils which is, in fact, scientifically hygenic, although I assure you the flavour of charcoal is not very pleasant, and as for washing well many for five or six months of the year just don't. Fortunately I may say all the pupils appear to wash frequently, although I daresay some will cease to do so if the situation becomes serious. The camels' milk diet is one of the things that astonished us. Many of the interior people live solely on camel's milk, *nothing* else except maybe an occasional cup of *tea* in the so-called coffee shops, really just a circle of tree branches.

When they left the Somali Government put a jeep at their disposal for a final tour round the country as a gesture of thanks.

At the end of the school term the new Somali Director of Education was most eager that we should see that Somalia was not all desert. He went to great trouble putting a Land Rover at our disposal (the driver was one of the young reckless variety who delighted in leaving the track at the most unsuspected of moments to chase ostriches at 40 m.p.h.) for eight days, so that we could visit other districts. This is but an example of the appreciation shown us by the Somalis recently, even though the interior nomads, in the belief that all white men have gone, surreptitiously creep up to the driver to enquire who we may be.

It is among the scouts that I have made some of my best friendships. Most of the scouts are my pupils. The things we are doing with them no European, apparently, has done before, often they are astounded. They think that all Europeans are soft and drive around in cars all the time (as they do here) and are unable to walk. Consequently when we walk several miles with them or jump 'zariba' (hedges made with thorn branches) they receive some surprises. Now however they realise our capabilities, but the people in the town, especially the small street boys, find it extraordinary and whenever we are in the town with anyone you can guarantee a small crowd asking our 'hosts' inquisitive questions, for to talk to anyone or to ask questions of strangers is not considered bad manners.

In Thailand Alastair used his holidays to travel round visiting the homes of many of his pupils, and endearing himself to them in doing so. In a quiet way he was stepping over another frontier: outside Bangkok Britons were rarely seen travelling on buses, hitching lifts, or sleeping in humble village homes. In the capital both Thais and Britons would have been agitated and alarmed had they known some of the risks he took — and undoubtedly he did take risks. But no fresh breakthrough in any field of human endeavour is ever accomplished by sitting at home in safety and comfort; Alastair and the other volunteers in Thailand did, by their willingness to accept as normal the local standards of living, undoubtedly open up a new dimension in East-West relationships.

The holidays were only for ten days and there were several things which I had thought of doing. I hoped to take a party of boys somewhere but then I found that, although they would like to come with me, they thought that they should go home to visit their family as most of them had been away for three months. Many of the boys had invited me to go to their homes during the holidays and it seemed too good a chance to miss. Very few Europeans are ever asked to go to a Thai home, because the Thais are usually too embarrassed about the state of them. I decided to make my way up to the north to visit some friends.

I spent the first night in Bangkok as the train to the north

YOUNG THAI

left very early next morning. I slept in a house, or should I say a room, belonging to some distant aunt of Sopon who was the student who was going to take me to Nakon Sawan. The house was situated in one of the Chinese slum areas and so you can imagine there were about ten people sleeping in one room. I must say I could not have slept better lying on the floor with a blanket (quite chilly as it was then the winter season), but the most amusing thing would have been to see me washing myself with my 'pakama' on, and then taking the wet one off and putting the dry one on. To begin with I was rather clumsy at this operation but I have now progressed so that I can manipulate my pakamas with grace.

On Saturday morning we met some of the other students at the station and we all set off together in a rather crowded train, to say the least. We arrived at Nakon Sawan at about lunch time and for the rest of the afternoon I was hauled round to their old schools and to their friends to be exhibited like a prize pig. As you will realise they thought they were very important to have a 'farrang' with them and they made sure that everyone should see me.

That evening they took me to the town fair (December is the season of fairs) and it was really very enjoyable as there was a beautiful display of Thai dancing. Eventually we got to bed by 12.30 a.m. and I was to be up at 4 a.m. to catch the bus for Lampang which left at 5 a.m. That night I slept at Nakon Sawan with another student, because he insisted I should sleep in his hovel as I had slept the night before with Sopon. I had originally planned to go to Lampang by train to visit my friends and the Nakon Sawan students said they would accompany me. But

200

we found that the train was unsuitable as it would take too long and so I would have to travel by bus if I was to reach my friends in time. Sopon and Sunai then said they had to stay at home to help their fathers, but I think the truth was that they were frightened by the thought of the bus trip. I should say now that the buses, which are converted from lorries by putting some seats and a covering to make it as comfortable as possible, drive at the most terrifying speed of about 65–70 m.p.h. People sit on the roof, hang from the sides, and of course there are no such things as tickets. As you can imagine accidents happen fairly frequently, but down here in the Central Plain they are not very serious as the bus just rolls into the klong and the passengers get a soaking. But in the North it is a different story where there are hills, because the buses plunge down into the gulleys bringing death to everyone. There had been such an accident only a few days before and I think it shattered my friends' confidence in the buses for a week or two.

So I set out from Nakon Sawan, which is in the north of the Central Plain, at 5 a.m. by bus and arrived at Lampang at 4 p.m. It was one of the most enjoyable days I have had because I made so many new friends, also because the scenery was so beautiful. We travelled up through the forests near the Burmese border and it was one of the most thrilling moments I can remember when I saw my first elephants lumbering along the side of the road.

Everyone in the bus was so kind that they were offering me fruit having only known me for a few minutes, and before the bus reached Lampang I knew nearly everyone in it. When we stopped at a small village for lunch I dined with the bus driver and his mechanics, and I must relate a small incident with the former which was rather amusing. When we stopped at the Yung Tee Dam, which is an American project, the windscreen shattered, with the heat I think. When we started again you can imagine the red dust which came flying through at us as the roads are unsurfaced, and the driver was driving with one hand on the wheel and the other over his face. I really thought there was going to be an accident because he was taking a corner with a drop of a hundred feet on one side at 65 m.p.h., with one hand, and although I enjoyed watching the skill I somehow felt responsible for the others in the bus. I decided something had to be done and so I offered to tie my handkerchief over his mouth and nose to let him concentrate with both hands. He thought it a terrific idea and eventually this masked cowboy managed to get his stagecoach to Lampang in one piece.

Here I managed to contact my students and once more I was taken to all their homes so that I could meet all their families. This town was rather delightful and it reminded me of Austria, because instead of rickshaw-tricycles they had carriages drawn by ponies. In the north it is much colder and here everyone was wearing greatcoats as it was winter.

The next morning we, that is a few of my students who live in Lampang, went up to Chiengmai which is called the 'Bangkok of the north', and here we spent a night in a hostel. The train had to climb up and down hills through teak forests and it really was beautiful country. All students think Chiengmai is the most wonderful place, and this is only because the women have a fairer complexion. I was disappointed with the town, but the villages surrounding it are really beautiful and the inhabitants are almost as kind as the ones at Sampran. During our stay here we saw the famous temples and also the highest waterfall in Thailand. At school everyone raved about this waterfall, which turned out to be only about twenty feet high, but of course I admired it with awe. It is only natural that a waterfall is something of exquisite beauty to a Thai as the majority of them live in the Plain and have never seen one.

My friends proved excellent guides as they had plenty of friends to visit and knew Chiengmai very well. We eventually left in the afternoon and arrived back in Lampang for dinner. That night I travelled down to Pitcanoloke and arrived there at 3 a.m., hoping to be met by a student. But he had forgotten, so I just went to sleep on the platform much to the amusement of everybody.

At 6.30 a.m. I got a bus out to my friend's village and when I arrived I found there were flags all round the house. On enquiring Suebrak said that it was his sister's wedding and that I was just in time for the ceremony. I had previously been to a wedding in Bangkok, but this village one outdid it by miles as it started at 6 a.m. and finished at 8.30 p.m.

I was just in time to see the orange-robed monks making the water holy by passing a bit of string through their clasped hands, then to the water, then to the image of Buddha and finally round the house. The water having been made holy, then a loop of string was placed on top of the bride and bridegroom's head and tied. After a series of chants they became man and wife and then all the guests had to pour holy water on their hands to wish them happiness.

When the monks had eaten, then all the guests were given a breakfast of Chinese food. After this followed an invasion of the bridegroom's friends who brought ducks and pork, which I think is a Chinese custom. Before they could enter the house they had to bargain a price with the mistress of the house, who stood in front of the entrance with a chain to bar the way. As you know the Thais love any ceremony and this was no exception with shouting, brass bands, and with water and flour being thrown around. In the afternoon when the others were having a rest, Suebrak got a forestry friend to take us out to the forest where I again saw some waterfalls and elephants.

Then at 4.30 p.m. another feast began, this time outside the bridegroom's house and every male in the village had been invited. That night all the relations stayed and there must have been at least seventeen of us all stretched on the floor. The next day I returned to Bangkok with a friend.

On paper my six-day trip may look to you like a tourist excursion, but I can assure you it has been of the greatest use. Firstly the boys at whose homes I stayed were all thrilled and are still talking about it. Even the other boys are pleased that I have stayed in Thai homes, and now they wish to take me to their homes. But what was invaluable was the number of new friends which I made and with whom I exchanged addresses and who have written to me since. It was encouraging to me, in a selfish way, that many of them had shown a little hostility at the sight of a 'farrang', but then when we parted we were the best of friends.

I can always detect hostility at once because Thais are always too emotional to hide anything. I then make up my mind that I shall do everything possible to communicate with him. First of all it is no good to go up and say in Thai, 'How do you do? I wish to speak with you,' because the shell closes tighter. One must just wait for an opportunity to come and then one must do a kind act or else make a joke at your own expense. If you are on a bus it is easy enough to do the former because you give up your seat for anyone and insist on sitting on the floor, which pleases everyone except me as it puts out of place every bone in my body. The other thing to do is, instead of paying the fare with two crisp notes to have a handful of coins (equivalent of $\frac{1}{2}$d. or $\frac{3}{4}$d.) and to pay one by one saying that I am a poor farrang. The Thais like this as they are amused by anything as long as it is not plugged too long. All the time I watch my marked man who will always listen and suddenly he looks at me and smiles. I smile back and I know I have won. He will then take the initiative and ask me something, and we talk away until it is time to leave. Of course the Thais love when I try my little knowledge of Thai and it pleases them that I should have tried to learn. My Thai is not as good as I would like it to be, as I have made a rule to speak English always in school with the boys, but I know enough to be able to communicate with someone, which I suppose is the main thing.

My policy in Thailand is to trust everyone and everything, including any water which I may see, or even dogs, which Thais regard as the lowest form of life, perhaps because there are so many cases of rabies. The kind of remark I hear in Bangkok is, 'always take the number of the taxi before you enter.' I am beginning to believe sincerely that there is goodness in all men, and that one must trust everyone if you wish them to trust you. How do I put this into practice? Well, often I have been in Bangkok in the evening and I am unable to get back to Sampran by bus as the last one leaves at 7 p.m., so I just go to the outskirts, wait for the first truck to come and stick out my hand. It will always stop, and the driver and mechanic are so surprised that I trust them that they are too thrilled for words to think about coshing me. I say this quite seriously as the truck drivers are renowned for their dishonesty and for jumping passengers, they are also the main carriers of opium. When we reach Sampran I always stand them a meal at the small food stall, and we say goodbye to each other like brothers.

CHAPTER VI

The End

DERMOT

So, inevitably, it came to an end. The year that twelve months ago had seemed to stretch, unknown and frighteningly exciting, towards an unseen horizon was suddenly experienced; its dimensions were precisely defined. Almost overnight the volunteer found himself looking backwards instead of forwards, no longer planning for the future but assessing what was already past.

We, too, looked back over the year, to learn from it the lessons that would be helpful to the next batch of youngsters waiting apprehensively in the wings. For them the emphasis which we placed on their predecessors' work could be all important in establishing their attitude of mind and setting their priorities. We felt strongly, and results justified us in so feeling, that it was in a way of living rather than in a kind of doing that the volunteer made his real contribution. The core of his year, the yardstick of his success, lay in his capacity for friendship in many different forms.

There are those who maintain that no volunteer going overseas for a short period has any right to become involved personally in the lives of those with whom he works. Both for his own sake and for others he should remain detached and efficient, doing a worthwhile job but leaving no kind of vacuum when he returns. I feel this attitude to be a false one, based on misconceptions about the nature of man, particularly young man, and the realities of time. It is not more efficient ways of doing jobs that the world most desperately needs, it is the fulfilment of the basic Christian commandment to love ones neighbour as ones self. The strings that may eventually draw the world closer together are not those attached to parcels of economic aid but the heart strings which join men of different countries in a common affection. In this time was unimportant, what mattered was the intensity of the experience and the degree of involvement. Many of us have known our whole lives to be affected by contacts which, in terms of time, were very slight.

This being our standpoint we made it clear to the volunteers that they took the whole of themselves overseas holding nothing back. It was here that their youth was their great advantage: the springs of affection were still unblocked and they were ready to open their hearts to other people and to enter into their lives. They had not yet become suspicious or wary of motives — and it was surprising what a difference a year or two could make in this respect. For the first time many of them found themselves among peoples who were, in a real sense, socially alive and integrated, and they recognised with surprise that much of the life in their own country, with its guarded non-involvement, was in essence anti-social. The warmth of the casual greetings on the streets, the open cheerfulness of the flashing smiles from strangers, the hospitality which took no thought of time or inconvenience but shared without embarrassment whatever was in the house, all this made a deep impression. And the uninhibited openness of their response was appreciated and valued by peoples who were unaccustomed to such simple acceptance of their friendship by Westerners. A volunteer wrote from Nigeria:

The difficulty is to rise up to their level. They are allegedly 'primitive', 'backward', etc. but I feel that there is a lot in their life and attitude which our 'civilisation' has destroyed, for which we should be sorry. Their sense of humour is marvellous, their willingness and eagerness to learn, is something quite new to me, and their loyalty and completely overwhelming trust, friendship and hospitality something that we, unfortunately, seem to have lost.

There was a whole changed attitude of mind here, a readiness to admit that working together benefited both sides which had not been a noticeable characteristic of those who had gone out in previous generations. There was little feeling among the volunteers that the giving was all on their side, except in one important and fundamental way. Because of their youth they felt that all they really had to give was themselves, and this, in the end, was the only thing that really mattered. Because they were prepared to take risks in the giving of themselves, to step out of their background and stand as people before other people, open to receive as well as to give, because of this relationships began to be forged which had a different flavour to them from the kind of relationships that had gone before. Of course it was on a small scale, of course there were lapses and failures, but the volunteers recognised the ideal and were not content when they failed to reach it.

Early on in the experience there began the first critical glances back at their homeland. One wrote from North Borneo:

> I have found people here infinitely more generous and sympathetic than people in England. A Chinese boy in England is treated no better (in fact often worse) than a local boy, but here every adult friend treats me like a son. It is really quite moving. No trouble is too great for them to make me happy.

There may have been naivety here, and the first rapture was soon overlaid by the everyday problems of daily living. That particular volunteer felt his year to have been a failure and wrote before he left in a different vein.

> I leave with a great deal of sadness because I know that I have not succeeded. I have built up a good deal of opposition to myself, often for petty reasons. I have been too reserved, and that side of myself which I know is there but I can never force out, has not appeared.

But the humility and the recognition of other's qualities and of his own failings did not go unnoticed. He became a human being to those among whom he worked, and not, as had so often happened in the past, a symbol or a representative whose heart and thoughts remained a mystery.

The out-going spirit which they all shared, not as a mission, but because it was fun to discover, to step across boundaries, to penetrate barriers, led them to accept invitations from all sides, and having accepted to immerse themselves in whatever was provided. It was Sari in Malaya who, although she worried about getting fat, always ate without question whichever of the many varied national dishes was set before her.

> I am always being told that I must be careful what I eat as it is so easy to get tummy upsets; while I appreciate these cautionary words I can't enquire into the source of food I eat every time I'm out with my friends. It seems to me that the people who get the most frequent tummy upsets are those who eat European food and only occasionally the local dishes.

She was not the only volunteer to recognise the importance of this matter of food, and to realise that in this, as in other ways, risks must be taken. In hospitality the under-developed world has much to teach the affluent society, and to reject the food provided, however tactfully, was an affront to friendship and human dignity. To reject, that is to say, on the grounds that it might be dirty or diseased, not suitable for civilised stomachs. From Sierre Leone another youngster wrote:

> It is very true of Africa that to know more of the people one must go into their houses and eat what they eat, drink what they drink. However this presents problems sometimes! On one occasion I played an away match with the Northern Province cricket team. The dinner that they served up was so peppery that even the locals complained about it. I managed to get some down me with a jug of water in one hand, which they had to fill up twice. Since that day I have been welcomed wherever I go.

Because there were no family trammels the volunteers kept open house, and enjoyed the constant stream of friends that

NIGERIAN BABY

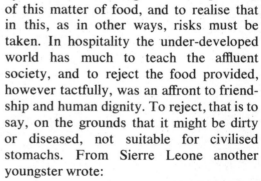

passed through their rooms. Sometimes these visits were the source
of mutual enlightenment. There were Mr Liew and Mr Shun the two
jolly bachelors who lived next door to Fred and Sean.

We teach them English for an hour every night and they teach
us Chinese every other night. We get on very well and have fun
with each other's pronunciation. Every now and then Mr Shun
lets out a loud strangled sound, 'EUEUEUEUEUEUEU'
risking imminent rupture of the throat and all four of us go into
peals of laughter.

Often the visits were a revelation to the volunteer as well as
to his pupils.

It is not often that I do not have a house full of boys in the
evenings, extremely interested in my belongings. They discuss
everything with complete frankness and are free from any inhibitions whatever. In reciprocation I find my own natural,
I suppose English, reserve vanishing rapidly.

A number of volunteers, going to countries which were in the
throes of political struggle, had half-steeled themselves to meet
hostility and were surprised by the unforced friendliness of the
ordinary people, who greeted them on every side without strain
or insincerity. Occasionally indeed the greeting was particularly
warm because they were British and, in spite of all differences,
somehow part of the family. One young man in Bechuanaland,
visiting a strange district during the holidays, found himself
surrounded by his pupils whose home it was.

It has been wonderful to meet my own students who insist
I go home to meet their families and introduce me to everyone
on the street—'That is our teacher, all the way from London,'
and then add the delightful touch—'he is not a Dutchman!'

This friendliness towards the single volunteer was noticeable
everywhere. The arrival of one young man, obviously still a boy,
brought out a strong feeling of responsibility in the local people.
They recognised his nervousness, his need for help, and responded
to it with warmth. No solitary volunteer in a completely indigenous
situation was likely to suffer from loneliness or hostility. The difficulties in this way were increased, paradoxically, as the number of
volunteers in any one project rose. An African or Asian headmaster

and staff generally felt nothing but liking for their one expatriate helper; he presented no threat to them and he needed their companionship and assistance. The moment that there were two volunteers this situation became less likely. Naturally they were thrown together – and this too could have dangers in that they might grow to be jealous of or to dislike each other – they lived together and a sensitive or insecure headmaster was aware that they probably discussed him together and feared that they did so adversely. Inevitably the relationship was more wary, more full of tensions.

For the volunteer too there were advantages in solitude. He was aware that there were relationships to be established, he wanted to get involved, but the first steps were often not so easy and, like a nervous bather, he could wrap himself in his native reserve and stand shivering on the brink. This was all the easier to do if he had, in any case, another volunteer with whom he could make friends and who could provide some kind of a buffer between himself and the unknown world of non-European friendship. But if that buffer was not present then he was forced, if he were not to appear to himself as a total failure, to take the plunge, to involve himself in the only life there was, the local life around him. And because this plunge had to be taken immediately, almost without time for consideration, he was, again like the bather, swimming strongly almost before he realised it.

With involvement there came first the recognition that men everywhere share certain common human virtues and failings quite regardless of their colour, and then very often admiration, born of understanding. One volunteer wrote from Southern Africa:

> Only now, when I see some of the difficulties which confront these fellows, do I realise how fortunate I have been in having had a good, free education and in living in a truly democratic

AFRICAN HILLS

country. I don't think any European can ever really understand the hardships through which an African boy goes in order to get an education. One 'boy' (he's twenty-three) in the top form works on the principle of one year's labour, two years schooling.

And Michael in Malaya, wrestling in his orphanage with the problems of outcast and underprivileged boys, came passionately to defend their cause, a passion which was to make him change his original career in order to train as a teacher so as to continue the fight.

I feel they are all worthy of the opportunity to be educated if that opportunity can, by any possible means, be made available. I have come to realise the rate at which these under-developed parts of the world are being transformed into civilised territories and how urgently these boys should be armed to cope with the transformation in the years to come.

Friendship and understanding grew up out of hard work and problems faced together. No amount of sightseeing or conscious fraternising could have produced the wholehearted allegiance to their new country and their new friends that sharing in the day to day difficulties did. Affection and liking were often the by-products of mutual co-operation, sometimes surprising the volunteer himself for the work was not always easy and to know people is not necessarily to like them.

Holiday expeditions, when classroom tensions were relaxed, were often a source of greater understanding. Sean wrote:

One of the best things (about the expedition) was their friendship which revealed itself in ways which were at first a trifle embarrassing for an Englishman brought up under the principles of stiff upper lip and never-show-your-emotions school of thought. Once they had accepted us they would fling their arms round our shoulders while we walked with them. They never got so far as to hold our hands, which is what they do when walking with a close friend, which is perhaps just as well for us. After a bit I got used to having a six-footer with his arm round me (though I must say I never felt less like a schoolteacher, completely dwarfed as I was) but I doubt if I could ever have felt comfortable holding hands!

211

I enjoyed the holiday and it did a lot to our relations with the boys. Up to then we had been getting to know them one by one, but in that holiday we got to know about twenty of them very well. We had to, as we were living with them, sleeping on the same floors with them and eating the same meals as they were.

Although the volunteers generally found it easier to put their practical achievements into words than to write about the more subtle and delicate subject of personal relationships, their sense of priorities, where these two things were concerned, was never in doubt. In Sarawak Ian remarked:

I still divide my time between games supervision, extra curricular science activities and idle chatter. Although it could never be called exacting work I think that the 'idle chatter' may be the most important of the three. The boys are continually amazed over my views on so many subjects, and I find their views, especially about 'civilisation', so difficult to understand that I think we both learn a great deal.

In the Solomon Islands John, also attempting to discuss views of civilisation, wrote back a warning to future volunteers.

I would like to stress the one word 'photos'. Photographs of your family, house, garden, street, interior rooms, town, country, farms, milk floats, buses, trains, rows of shops, etc., etc. They are extremely keen to learn exactly how English people live, so magazines showing houses and rooms, etc., e.g. 'Home', are invaluable. One photo I wish I had is of a traffic jam, and a picture of a crowd at a football match, in the street, especially Oxford Street on Christmas Eve. Just how do I get them to picture that in my home town, in sixteen square miles, are 180,000 people, more than in all the Solomons?

WOOD CARVER

Some years later I heard a girl, who had served as a volunteer in the Far East, describe her experiences and was very struck by her conclusion. 'I think,' she said 'that because we were the same age as the students we gave them, for the first time, a chance to reject certain Western values if they so wished and this was extremely important.'

Although most volunteers accepted at once the country to which they were accredited this was not always or automatically the case. For many of them this first meeting with a land quite outside the European tradition was a catalytic experience and the immediate impact wiped out any lingering doubts which they may have had. There were, however, the few for whom this was not so and who, having steeled themselves for a painful year found after some months that their own outlook had undergone a change. Sometimes the alteration could be affected by a physical catastrophe—the hurricane in British Honduras acted in this way on one volunteer; sometimes a personal friendship, or the continuing influence of a climate of friendliness brought about a thaw. A very small minority left still disliking the country they had served in—only to surprise themselves by looking back with affection. In each case however what was important was that the volunteer knew at the outset that, whatever he might find on arrival, there was no turning back, and so there was time for circumstances to work a change.

One of the volunteers in British Honduras thought very poorly of that country when he arrived. Coming himself from a sophisticated and cultured background it seemed dead to the world outside, with a people who were idle and self-satisfied. He prepared for a miserable year and decided that the only way to fill it was to do the work that had to be done as efficiently and wholeheartedly as he could without letting himself think of much else.

A month later a hurricane hit Belize which brought all normal work to a standstill and created problems of such magnitude that there was no time to think of personal unhappiness. Houses were wrecked, thousands left homeless, food was short, disease probable, the town in chaos; the school in which he worked was virtually destroyed and over everything in the first days brooded a spirit of depression and fear.

Out of this experience, as work to put the town back on its feet gained momentum, the volunteer found that his whole attitude towards its people had changed. In their acceptance of the disaster and their attitude towards each other and himself he began to discover a kindliness and simplicity and friendliness which charmed him. The tempo of living, which in its slowness had originally so annoyed him, was still there—but now he began to see it in a different light.

They are happy as they are, and surely that is better than anything. There cannot be any comparison between what people are like here and what they would be like in a modern city. Belize has real character; even the open sewers do not have a wholly bad character! I wouldn't have it changed for any place in the world. It is odd that I only felt this recently. I can't think why I didn't feel it at first. I think the reason why I didn't think the people were friendly was probably because I wasn't too friendly myself. At first I used to go around in true English fashion trying to get a job done, and not caring about much else.

One has to realise that this is not England—obvious, but not all that easy. The people are accustomed to a much slower pace and are much friendlier. One never gets an invitation anywhere, one just goes; and there is always a welcome. The people like to sum up a stranger before they throw off their first reserve with him—especially if he is white. But once they think he is friendly they are the nicest people in the world. One *has* to hail them in the street, talk to them and go slow with them, instead of rushing off to the next job with one's head in the air.

Of course there is endless work to be done, but I would say that this is not the main purpose of a stay here. The main purpose is to get to know the people—to muck in with them—and not to boss them around. They are happy cheerful and content and they don't want any bossing around. They want friendship, and if it is friendship with a white man and an English person, their faith in England, justifiably at a fairly low ebb, will be reconfirmed.

He went on to describe something of the conditions under which people were living in the post-hurricane weeks and the attitude towards these conditions which aroused his admiration.

It is simply amazing how people are coping here now, for although things are superficially back to normal, in actual fact this is far from the case. The conditions under which people are living are simply appalling, and yet you never hear a word of complaint. I met a family about a month ago whom I have got

214

to know fairly well. At first it seemed all was fine with them and that they had not suffered as a result of the hurricane. Not a bit of it however. There are ten of them living together in a tiny little house in one of the most sordid areas of the town. There are two bedrooms, in one of which sleep the mother and father and two youngest daughters in one bed, and the four eldest daughters on one mattress, and in the other the oldest daughter, her husband and their baby. And that family is comparatively well-off. But never a word of complaint, and they act as if nothing has happened.

A capacity for admiration was one of the endearing qualities of the volunteers, and it is not a quality for which youngsters are always given credit these days. They were capable of and expressed openly their respect not only for many of those among whom they lived, but also very often for those of their own countrymen with whom they worked. Letters frequently arrived expressing gratitude for having been able to work under such a leader, and this close personal contact with men of initiative and courage often had an effect on the volunteer's own plans for his future. Among the school-leavers the number who wished to return overseas was very high.

Unlike the school-leaver, however, the apprentice returned to the same job from which he had gone out, and for him the major problem of the year occurred when this return was due. He came back to the work bench, sometimes having lost seniority to the friends whom he had left behind; often he felt that no one was particularly interested in his experience overseas or understood what it had meant to him, and it could be that those with whom he worked directly went out of their way to make it plain to him that he was not such a fine fellow after all. The school-leaver volunteered for a year at a moment of change in his career, and he came back to the new experience of college or job which helped him over the transition period. Not so the apprentice, for whom life could suddenly become routine and flat.

This resulted in a high rate of defections among those who came from industry, and it was interesting to find that many of those who felt impelled to leave their firms did so to go into the church or become lay missionaries. This happened to Phil who, when he had married the girl who had waited for him, took her back to the

215

Cameroons to serve in one of a mission's settlements for lepers. David also found Manchester intolerable after Nairobi and he join-ed the Merchant Navy. This was not a problem capable of easy solu-tions, but it opened up a fascinating field of sociological speculation.

As the end came in sight many were surprised to find that they were going to be the recipients of farewell gifts. It was not only William who came proudly home the possessor of a colourful local costume. Chris, also in West Africa, described how,

> the senior female student, almost petrified with nervousness, presented me with a beautiful full-length gown on behalf of all the students. Those who yelled 'Put it on!' and 'Speech' were gratified, though my two minute speech could express little of what I wanted to say, and I think I would have had great difficulty in putting my feelings into words.
>
> The gown is of damask, dyed locally, and must have cost them all of £6, which is a lot for one hundred students of very limited income. The dance lasted until two o'clock in the morning and I demonstrated my 'skill' in the 'high life' many times. I finally got to bed at three and was up again at six to see them off at the station. As the train pulled out I don't mind confessing that there was quite a lump in my throat. They were always so pleased to see me and as eager to learn about me as I was to learn about them.

Perhaps that was as good an end as any to this creative year.

FRIENDS

361   D561   C 1

DICKSON M

WORLD ELSEWHERE VOLUNTARY S

IUP LIBRARIES

A000003542156

RHOD   RARY

INDIA   PA.

Cuba

Cayman Is.　Haiti　Dominican Rep.

Puerto R

Jamaica

Labrador

Cayman Is.
Br. Honduras　Jamaica
Br. Guiana　Gambia
Sierre Leone

Be

Falkland Is.

West Falkland　East Falkland

S. Atlantic　Falkland Is.